# Sharing Our Stories

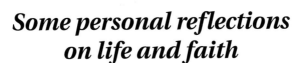

*Some personal reflections
on life and faith*

Compiled and edited by Cynthia and David Capey
for Suffolk Inter-Faith Resource

British Library Cataloguing in Publication Data

Printed in England  by POSTPRINT
Snetterton Business Park, Snetterton, Norfolk NR16 2JZ

Compiled and edited by Cynthia and David Capey
for Suffolk Inter-Faith Resource
The Inter-Faith Centre
The West Building
University Campus Suffolk
Waterfront Building
Neptune Quay
Ipswich, Suffolk, IP4 1QJ


Email: office@sifre.org.uk
Website: www.sifre.org.uk


Suffolk Inter-Faith Resource is a Charitable Company
Company Number: 2992865
Registered Charity: 1042612
Registered in England and Wales

### "The Walking Madonna"

A sculpture by Elizabeth Frink. It is positioned outside Salisbury Cathedral. Mary, as an older woman, is shown striding purpose-fully away from the cathedral. It is a thought-provoking symbol as it challenges us to set out from our comfort zones and embark on journeys with an open heart and mind, not knowing whom we might meet along the way.

# Contents

# Preface

In 1992, SIFRE published its first book, 'Faiths in Focus in Ipswich and Suffolk', which contained general information about the faith communities present in the county. In 1994, it was followed by a second book, 'Finding our Way and Sharing our Stories' which, by contrast, was composed of personal stories written by women, reflecting on their lives in the light of their traditions. These books were able, between them, to give an overview of religious groups as a whole, while also allowing individuals to speak for themselves, thus challenging the simple generalisations which can lead to stereotyping. Twenty years later it is time to return to the task.

This 'Sharing our Stories' is a collection of more than 50 personal accounts by individuals, both men and women, of their lives and their beliefs. Some have lived all their lives in Suffolk, some have settled here for various reasons and others have come here to work or study. However, their stories highlight some of the experiences and challenges that face everyone in our diverse society, including issues of gender, disability, race, persecution and displacement. It also reveals the struggles individuals may have in maintaining their integrity with regard to their faith and spirituality.

People are often asked to state their religious affiliation and some are happy to be categorised in this way as Bahá'ís, Buddhists, Christians, Hindus, Jains, Jews, Muslims, Pagans, Sikhs, Taoists and Zoroastrians (all represented in Suffolk).

There are many others who see themselves as outside these boxes and their voices can also be heard through these stories.

The process of collecting the articles was complicated by the fact that some of the contributors became so absorbed in the task that they found themselves writing a full life story. Others had to be cajoled to get started! The result is a rich mix of articles of varying lengths and styles from people of different ages and with many different backgrounds and roles in society.

Alongside this anthology of individual stories there is an evolving collection of general articles about the faith communities of Suffolk, their history, beliefs and practices, contemporary concerns, places of worship and contact details. This is available on-line at **www.sifre.org.uk**

*SIFRE is grateful to all those who openly or anonymously give their time to work with us on our various projects. We thank the contributors to this anthology, those who have helped with the shaping of the material and especially Margaret Nelson for her extensive proof reading. We look forward to further co-operative work with all our friends of various faiths, beliefs and philosophies.*

# The importance of inter-faith encounters

The population of Britain is becoming increasingly multi-cultural and multi-faith. This may not be apparent in rural areas, but in towns and cities, people of many different faiths live side by side, and places of worship for minority faiths, often converted from other uses, are proliferating. This can cause anxiety in the wider population and can lead to social disturbances and acts of violence.

It is very important, therefore, that people of all faiths work together to build a society based on shared values. The Inter-Faith Network for the UK has set out guidelines for this.

They include:

- Respecting other people's freedom within the law to express their beliefs and convictions,
- Learning to understand what others actually believe and value, and letting them express this in their own terms,
- Recognising that all of us fall short of the ideals of our own traditions and never comparing our own ideals with other people's practices.

There are many values which people of faith hold in common. At the heart of these is the Golden Rule which is found in various forms, as for example in Hinduism – "This is the sum of duty: do not do to others what would cause pain if done to you."   *Mahabharata 5:1517*

This simple rule is a good foundation for human society, but the world's religions agree on so much more in principle:

- Community, personal integrity,
- A sense of right and wrong,
- Learning, wisdom and love of truth,
- Care and compassion, justice and peace
- Respect for one another,
- For the earth and its creatures.

*from the Statement of Commitment of Faith Communities of the UK at the beginning of the New Millennium*

In reality, however, conflict arising from religion has been at the heart of many wars, has led to persecutions and acts of oppression and terrorism. Conflicts have occurred over holy places, sacred texts, beliefs and doctrines, rituals and leadership.

In recent years there have been many movements, both national and international, to confront this age-old human problem, including: The World Conference for Religions for Peace, The World Parliament of Religions, The World Congress of Faiths, The Inter Faith Network UK, The Council of Christians and Jews, The Three Faiths Forum, The United Religions Initiative, and many more. Alongside these, there have been endeavours on a smaller scale, local inter-faith groups and grass roots movements, which complement and support the bigger networks, and even in some cases challenge them. It is very easy for national and international organisations to become institutionalised and create rigid boundaries which can exclude others who would be fellow travellers. It is up to individuals to find the courage and the love to cross the boundaries.

As Edwin Markham wrote:

> He drew a circle that shut me out
> Heretic rebel, a thing to flout
> But love and I had the wit to win
> We drew a circle that took him in.

Cynthia Capey,
from *Facing the Issues* (published by Kevin Mayhew, 2012)

# Suffolk 2014: A Faith Profile

The religious make-up of Suffolk is diverse and changing, and while it is possible to gain an overall view, it is easy to stereotype the various groups, or to confuse culture with faith. The census for 2011 lists 443,632 Christians in Suffolk but there are numerous Christian denominations. These include Anglican (Church of England), Baptist, Christadelphian, Christian Scientist, Church of Jesus Christ of Latter-day Saints (Mormons), Congregational, German Lutheran, Greek Catholic, Greek Orthodox, Celtic Orthodox, Independent Pentecostal, Jehovah's Witnesses, Methodist, Roman Catholic, Russian Orthodox, Salvation Army, Society of Friends (Quakers), Seventh-Day Adventist, Unitarian, United Reformed Church, and various Independent and house churches. There are also members of eastern churches, like Syrian Orthodox, Copts and Armenians, among the asylum seekers and refugees in Suffolk, and the migrant workers from Poland and Portugal have swelled the numbers of Roman Catholics.

Alongside these diverse Christian groups there are Bahá'ís (around 40), Buddhists (2,094), Hindus (2,274), Humanists, Jains, Jews (677), Muslims (5,818), Pagans (600), Sikhs (626), Taoists and Zoroastrians. However, these figures omit the statistics of some faiths and underestimate others. Significantly they do not show the different paths within each faith. There are several strands of Buddhism in Suffolk – Triratna Buddhists, Tibetan Buddhists, and SGI Buddhists, Thich Nhat Hanh followers and various others – who may or may not meet together regularly. Muslims in Suffolk, originally mostly from Bangladesh, now come from all around the world and include significant numbers of Kurds, Iraqis and Afghans.

The greatest diversity of faiths is found in Ipswich, which has many religious buildings including, alongside the churches, 3 mosques, a Sikh Gurdwara, a Buddhist centre and a Hindu mandir. The Suffolk Liberal Jewish Community meets regularly and celebrates its festivals in various premises, including those of the Salvation Army. There is an Ipswich Pagan Council representing the many Pagan paths followed in the county. People from minority faiths can be found throughout the county – for example, the 2011 census recorded 209 Buddhists, 152 Muslims, 78 Jews and 17 Sikhs in Mid-Suffolk District, which is largely rural.

In Lowestoft, Bury St Edmunds, and Newmarket, sizeable groups of Muslims meet for Friday prayer; there are at least two mosques in Newmarket, including one within the racing stables, and small groups of Muslims meet together in other towns, such as Sudbury, especially during Ramadan. Some faith groups may hire rooms when needed or meet in members' homes. Hindus, Buddhist and Sikhs may well have family shrines or prayer rooms within their houses. In Lowestoft the population has become more mixed through the presence of refugees, migrant workers and maritime students from around the world, and Bury St Edmunds (where the newly built tower of the Cathedral has been described as a spiritual beacon for the new millennium) is also becoming more diverse.

A wide representation of faiths is to be found in the prisons, supported by multi-faith chaplaincy teams; and in the hospitals and nursing homes, where the staff as well as the patients may come from a variety of faiths. BT frequently receives personnel on short contracts from overseas and people from many different faiths and cultures, speaking a great variety of languages, work in Suffolk factories. It is easy to overlook this group and their needs often go unmet, especially as they may be transported on a daily basis to factories in rural Suffolk and may have no contact with the local community.

There are people living amongst us from religious and cultural backgrounds who are not represented in this book, including Yazidis from Iraq. We need to hear their stories too.

# Abdullah Mawas: A perspective on Syria

I am a doctor working in West Suffolk Hospital, but my place of origin is a village in northern Syria between Aleppo and the border with Turkey. In a recent talk which I gave to a SIFRE dialogue group meeting in the West Suffolk Hospital chapel, I shared my experience of living in the Middle East, in a country that used to have good inter-faith relations. For centuries the religious make-up of the population of Syria has been mixed.

Before the present conflict the percentages in Syria could be broken down as follows: Muslims 85%, of which 85% were Sunni, 10% Alwites and 5% Shias; Christians made up 10% and included the Greek Orthodox Church of Antioch, the Melkite Greek Catholic Church, the Oriental Syriac Orthodox Church, the Armenian Apostolic Church and Eastern Catholic Churches; Druze accounted for 3% and there were also Jews, mostly in Aleppo and Damascus, either dating back to Biblical times or originating as colonies of refugees fleeing the Spanish Inquisition. There were several thousand Yazidis and also people with folk spiritual beliefs.

Syria's history has been one of invasion after invasion – by Egyptians, Phoenicians, Hebrews, Aramaeans, Assyrians, Babylonians, Persians, Greeks, Seleucids, Romans, Nabataeans, Byzantines, Muslim Arabs, European Christian Crusaders, Ottomans, Western Allied Forces and the French. However, Syria became independent on 11th April 1947 and until recently remained comparatively stable. The various communities lived together harmoniously.

In a Gallup poll taken in 2009, 87% of Syrians "agreed" or "strongly agreed" that they always treat members of other faiths with respect. 78% said they had a positive opinion of Christians and only 5% said they had a negative opinion.

In pre-conflict Syria, it was common for friends of other religions to attend each other's weddings and funerals, to mind each other's children and to give food to each other. It was considered rude to inquire into someone's religious background. In my opinion the Sunni/Shia dimension of the Syrian conflict had a greater basis in international rivalries than on the ground realities.

My Syrian brothers and sisters are now endangered. Villages and cities have been partially or completely destroyed. Medical facilities have been deliberately targeted and Syria is among the worst examples of targeting medical care as a weapon of war, as said by Donna McKay, executive director of Physicians for Human Rights.

I now work as a member of a multi-racial, multi-faith medical and nursing team at West Suffolk Hospital, in a place where community relations are peaceful. The contrast between this context and my place of origin could not be greater. Please hold my broken country and its neighbours in your hearts.

# Andrew Sterling: Uncovering Faith

Christianity and the figure of Jesus are part of the backdrop to my formative years. But my relationship to them became radically different as I gained experiences throughout life, especially dropping the former through a shift of focus towards the latter, which initially may seem puzzling.

I went to Sunday school, which included 'The Crusaders' who issued a lapel badge in the shape of a shield with a red cross. I attended church services from time to time -- always 'free' churches -- mainly Congregational. So I felt pretty comfortable in my teens when I volunteered to become a regular church organist at a local free church, called The Church Of Christ, not the Latter Day Saints, but a branch of the Congregationalists. Being a budding musician I confess my interest was primarily getting to play the organ.

Consequently I heard a fair few sermons, which regularly included commonly-heard phrases and words, such as "Son of God", "Redeemer", "Jesus died for our sins", "Saviour", "God/Jesus loves you" - and exhortations to have "faith". I didn't know what they were actually talking about and I wondered if they did either, as none of these terms were explained in any grounded way. But everyone round me seemed to accept them anyway – and I just took them as part of going to church and being a Christian. I tried to keep my quizzical feelings under my hat, not least in case the worshippers did actually know what they meant and I would make a fool of myself (this mattered when I was young and shy). But on occasion I would dare to question the orthodox outlook as I had strong antipathetical reactions to being expected to adopt others' assumptions, whatever they were – even if I agreed with them!

I eventually discovered that ideas and theories are a way of imposing templates on oneself, on others and on life. They put a handle on life so that we can have an understanding, but they are not life itself which, it seems to me, is viewable in an infinity of narrow ways, however true or false. I called this Pinhead Life – drawing down the infinite to a pinhead – the single view of a particular view/theory/religion. Life is so endlessly dimensional that all things point to wherever the viewpoint is and so that viewpoint looks like it is the centre. That was my theory anyway (and my personal experience)!

**How faith was uncovered – three main and other unexpected experiences.**

I had three main transformative experiences, spaced over at least forty years, plus a number of confrontational situations, and it was these, combined over this time, that produced in me a profound inner freedom and a previously unexperienced happiness and contentment – albeit in the midst of my still deeply troubled life in some respects, and a troubling world.

Each of these experiences occurred entirely unexpectedly, out of practical situations, not from study, debate – which I enjoy – or even contemplation.

The first happened when I was 22 years of age. I was filling in a year as a music teacher in an East End boys' school, in Bow, London. Unknown to me, the school was known as a 'sink' school – somewhere where boys were sent who couldn't be coped with elsewhere. It was very rough and challenging, especially to one as young and inexperienced as me. I was frightened and my stomach would be churning each Monday morning. The boys were often very damaged, some violent, some weird and unpredictable and some almost mute, and many a mix of these traits.

The regime in the school was like this; the boys either saw teachers as hard or as soft. If you were hard you whacked them with a cane (still legal and normal then) and generally behaved like the secret police. And sure, the boys were controlled by such teachers. Or, if you were seen as soft, then your life was made hell by the boys after the first week or two. Nervous breakdowns were not unknown amongst staff, and the previous music teacher had been found beaten up and unconscious in the music room – so I was told some time after I'd started there. One day, having stayed on after school to do some piano practice, I was walking down the narrow high-walled road from the school when I came across a group of boys on the other side of the road and I heard one say "Let's get him now," pause, then, "Nah, nah…" Phew!

The point is this; I haven't the personality to behave like a hard man or a softy. So I had riots—the chucking of chairs about, climbing out of the window, tipping up cupboards so that stuff went all over the floor. I had no alternative but to watch it.

I had no idea how my time there would turn out but, to cut the story very short, I gradually found that my non-reaction had the unintended effect of draining the boys of their need to riot – I wasn't giving any reaction they knew about. I neither caned them nor did I do a runner or plead with them, or indeed try to be nice. I had my sense of self-respect to look after.

After some time one boy (one of the worst there) told me they didn't understand me. I knew they didn't but for him to tell me was very significant. Indeed it turned out that was a turning point. After that the boys and I started to get on much better. By the end of the year the worst boys were my best mates. I was not only relieved but amazed. It was like a gift. Literally, I couldn't have designed it. The head, who originally thought I was useless, offered me head of department status if I would only come back after the summer holiday. I was sorely tempted because of what had happened, but in the end I decided to go to Paris for my music. But part of me still regrets not going back to that school and I still remember and think about those boys and I have wished and hoped the best for them.

It was this that gave me a life-long lesson: that under all that damage and aggression lies the real person waiting to respond to anyone who was just themselves, without a hidden or emotive agenda. Nature, then, is still there, waiting to manifest itself. And the thing is, it's stronger – because it's the underlying, real person – than the profoundly negative psychology the boys had as a result of the abusive and violent character of their lives.

My second transformative experience came after my marriage split up. This sort of experience tends to shock into the daylight any areas of difficulty with regard to one's relationship with the self which takes a bit of a bashing. And this is not something that one handles on one's own without a heap of self-delusion (I'm right, she's a bitch, I'm the injured person, she's ruining my life etc.). Having tried handling my emotions on my own I eventually realised I needed a professional third party. I was so fortunate in finding a particularly brilliant one (although I wasn't aware of this for some time).

It turned out to be a very long process. We cling onto ideas (delusions) and impressions that we all build up and through which we deal with everything and everyone else. It's what we know and understand about ourselves and life – it becomes part of our identity. Not that I had ever been aware of this dynamic of course, but I gradually became aware of it alright!

So initially it's liable to be a scary process; it can feel like the risk is that you are, after all, the pile of rubbish you had always unconsciously feared you were, and unconsciously avoided. I am told that many clients find it too challenging to face, and bow out. More than understood.

The thing is, there's no conception of a process or of particular outcomes. It is whatever it becomes. It is through this experience that you learn to trust it. You learn to relax and let go. Your anxiety to reassure yourself you are OK melts away. The process gradually dissolves the hanging onto your collated identity, ideas, defences and rationales and, eventually, allows a trust to manifest itself, that whatever you, and life, and others turn out to be is OK after all.

Like the East End boys, my inner nature was responding to this because I was getting out of the way and allowing it to emerge. What once had seemed the essence of fearful insecurity became inner freedom. I surprised myself one time by coming out with, "I had clung to the rocks that wrecked me." We'd rather cling to our destructive and negative behaviours and thoughts even though, underneath, we do know they are destructive, like smoking is, for an obvious example. But, in fact, most of our daily lives consist of fighting and rationalising an array of destructive habits/thought patterns.

My third transformative experience came through a camping and cycling holiday up the west coast of Ireland. The experience it gave me was – again -- utterly unexpected, especially as I really didn't want to go, but my daughter could see I needed a break and she made me go. It was only afterwards I realised the import of what had happened to me during that time.

I cycled and camped in unsophisticated campsites (what I think of as 'proper' camping) and I kept cycling and camping, cycling and camping. I simply became part of that process, and the process became part of me. That was all I did. Very simple. A week into this experience it dawned on me that what I needed had radically changed. I didn't want the things I usually look forward to; tea, eating, listening to music, etc. Out of anxiety (because I couldn't imagine I could do without it) I had taken a special flask to fill with tea to drink on my way. But to my bewilderment I found that tea tasted foul, even tea at a little teashop I tried at Galway Bay. So I filled the flask with water which was, for the first time in my life, tasting sweet. I was astonished. I found it hard to accept it was happening for real; perhaps I was imagining it? Likewise, I took a little radio too for entertainment and it simply became utterly irrelevant. And, though I was pumping out all that energy each day, I found I did not want to eat very much. I sometimes had to remind myself that I had better eat. It wasn't that I was full of amazing spurts of energy and joy, I was just on a steady, content plateau, and the psychological drive just to eat was missing.

Additionally – and I only realised it when I got back home – I hadn't done any thinking, i.e. conceptualising. I had no need to think what life meant, what I was, etc. I had no ambitions, no aims, no need to achieve anything, no judgements to make, or things I must consume or possess. I wasn't even aware I was content. A sense of happiness, I realised when I got home, comes with, and from, the contrast with a more underlying unhappiness.

Towards the end of my holiday I had a dilemma; the time had come to make my way home but I found my inner state was set to carry on, ad infinitum. I couldn't believe I had this prompting. My conscious self had to be harnessed (and it really was like that); don't be silly, I told myself, how can I camp through the winter? I also had work engagements to go back to as well.

It was when I gradually got into life back home that I realised I had been experiencing a natural dynamic for the first time; the interconnection between little concern for materialism/status with inner peace. Or, to put it the other way round, inner peace resulting in the absence of a need for the material and for status.

And conversely, as I got into the demands of contemporary life I also experienced a return to the comfort consuming, along with planning, hoping, wishing, ambition, and all the usual anxieties associated with them.

These changes happened to me, as autonomous processes, not the result of some planned idea or belief system, and this experience embedded itself in me transformatively (sub-consciously) and as revelatory (consciously).

These experiences have, together with positive outcomes when faced with confrontational situations that I've been in from time to time (to which I have reacted much like I did with the East End school boys), filled me from my inner core with a faith that we all have as a birthright.

We lose that inherent, experiential, faith early on in life through (I more than suspect) the lack of parental unqualified love and delight in how/who we are, regardless of expectations. They, the parents, had found it difficult because they themselves were similarly emotionally short-changed, as were their parents before them, and so on back through the generations (and forward too, of course).

These experiences showed me that Nature/God truly does know what we need. From that, and from the underlying primitive emotions of the clever people I noticed, I took it that complex ideological, philosophical and theological thought is rationalisation, the outcome of our being out of touch with such experience. Such rationales are the substitute for the real thing, and would become largely irrelevant with the experience of the real thing.

So I reflect on the other species of the world who, I have to assume from their consistency, don't rationalise their realities: they are what they are, and they are what their functions are in the ecology. Yet within that I have found many animals are highly sentient, psychological, if not emotional, and can suffer nervous illness if they are living out of true with their natures too (as in the way we treat animals, as often our children, for our own spuriously rationalised ends).

But here's the conundrum; if it's impossible to have the experience of our true selves in the midst of our 'civilisation', then maybe such faith cannot take place?

Jesus' message was to the point; drop all things and live according to this faith. This chimed with my unexpected experience in Ireland. But in the context of our contemporary reality this message is bound to come over as unrealistic. Again, normality is reality, however destructive.

Yet, if we accept faith is not going to happen of its own subconscious accord within the context of this society, then there is a way we can find such faith, we can consciously engage with it. We can work at building an honest, trusting and listening relationship with ourselves, between ourselves and with life.

To avoid spending our lives responding to our emotive drives, the first step is to acknowledge that together that is precisely what we do.

In our 'uprooted' state we search for answers from a world of false realities, choices and drives. We develop belief systems to tie life down, to make it feel certain, predictable and to build hope. But it continues to feel all the more insecure, like a tarpaulin flapping in the wind, because life, of course, is what it is and so it will keep disappointing our preconceptions and hopes.

And, coming with different backgrounds and particular emotional deprivations, we come with different ideas with which to try to tie life down. So our different ideas conflict, and as we are tempted to insist that our own beliefs and perspectives are the right ones, because we emotively need them to be, they are, by definition, misleading, however factually supported they may be, or can be made to be.

Instead we need to discern the fundamental difference between the 'letting go' faith and what is making it up; i.e. what we want to believe. I have tried to express this in the following way:

- Faith is the absence of belief and dogma.
- Dogma and belief are the absence of faith.
- Faith has no name; beliefs have names.
- Faith accepts; belief rejects.
- Faith is not about being right or wrong; belief is about being right, by making other beliefs wrong.
- Faith is about letting go; belief interferes.
- Faith opens up; belief ties down.
- Faith trusts; belief distrusts.
- Faith allows; belief controls.
- Faith embraces; belief conflict.
- Faith accepts whatever the truth to be whatever it is, it is the reality whether it is seen or not.
- Belief is make-belief.
- Belief presents agendas as truth.

It seems, then, the spirit of faith that Jesus expressed has indeed finally made sense to me, over-riding doubts concerning the gospels, about authorship, the self-referencing agendas of the subsequent churches and translation inaccuracies which, together, create a mix rife with pitfalls, especially if the letter matters more than the spirit.

The apparent puzzles I couldn't get my head round and the seeming unreachable fantasy Jesus asked for have become profound insights of a wholly different and unexpected perspective.

This is why I don't see Jesus as professing a moral message. He wasn't telling people what they ought to do or believe or even how to behave. He wasn't telling people to be like this or that. That is 'behaving like'. Acting out. Shaping oneself. Engineering. All of which demonstrates an absence of faith. The morality/immorality spectrum exists in the absence of faith.

Faith is of a whole different order than that. Jesus was guiding, pointing the way, towards our inner birthright selves, towards what we already have in and between ourselves.

Life/nature/our heavenly father, does know what we need, and what we don't need, and we have to be in a listening, not assertive, mode to hear it, and for life to be allowed to work. This is faith.

# Aruna Mistry: A Hindu by birth

I moved to Ipswich in 1990 when I got married. I live with my husband, my mother-in-law, who is 84 years of age, and my son, who is 11 years old. I am a full time working mother and with an 11-year-old, most of my time just flies by each day. I am a Hindu by birth but I personally don't practise much! However my mother-in-law is a vegetarian and carries out prayers daily which last about an hour and a half!

At the age of 6, my family (including my brother, aged 1) came over from Africa to England in 1972. My mother spent most of her time looking after the family and also my granddad for 40 years. She tried to fulfil her duty as a daughter-in-law and a wife but she now feels bitter that she missed out on living her life the way she wanted to. I grew up in a working class family; my father worked in a factory making gas cookers and gas fires. He earned about £75 per week which he used to run the family, pay the mortgage and other bills and send money to his mother, who lived in India. We had no cars, fridge or telephones. Travelling was by using public transport and holidays were just spent visiting close family or entertaining them. We lived a simple life but a happy and healthy one! The main reason my parents came to England was so that myself and my brother could get a good education. Hence, both I and my brother studied hard to become educated up to at least degree level and we both got good jobs. After we started earning incomes, we brought a 3-bedroomed house, got a phone, a fridge and a car!

With regard to my current engagement/practice of being a Hindu; although I have a Hindu background, I don't feel I know much about Hinduism as a religion other than what I learned at school. As children, we certainly attended various Hindu festivals such as Holi, Navratri, weddings, pujas, New Year celebrations, etc., but we did not really understand their meaning and purpose. I suppose what I have learnt has really come from watching serials on television about the

Mahabharata, Ramayana, and Hanuman, etc. For me, Hinduism is an interesting religion but too complex to understand or put into practice. For one thing, there are too many gods and goddesses to learn about. However, I would say that I am spiritual and try to live life the right way, as a human being should.

I believe that there is only one God with many names so I respect all religions and am happy to attend any house of God whether it's a church, a temple or a mosque, etc. All religions have the same underlying message, so that's what I believe and understand. It is this principle which I am trying to teach my son.

Due to the previous lack of a vibrant Indian /Asian community in Ipswich, I have not really attended any Asian functions, except perhaps dinners and dance at Diwali, and with no Hindu temples (until recently), any worship was just done at home. I don't feel there has been much on offer in Ipswich until now regarding this matter, hence it has been very difficult for someone like my son to learn anything.

I believe that it's necessary to learn basic messages given in all religions so one can live a good life and conduct oneself correctly but it is not necessary to actually practise any particular religion or enforce one's views on anyone else. As long as you have a good heart, do not discriminate or judge anyone, do not harm anyone but love and respect all people of all religions, and try and help everyone when you can, then I think these are good principles upon which one can lead a good and happy life.

# Atul Shah: A Jain by culture

I am a Jain by culture, a word which few can spell. Even fewer have heard about Jainism, one of the oldest living religions of the world. I therefore belong to a minority group. As Indians are a minority, I am a minority within a minority. I have been living in this country for 25 years and have certainly encountered some prejudice. Visually, my complexion is black so I would stand out as different. Fortunately, affirming diversity is in my DNA, and as an Indian and a Jain, I have been brought up with an open mind and respect for other peoples, cultures and all living beings.

## Biodiversity is not a separate issue

Jainism does not restrict diversity to humanity, but sees the entire ecosystem as diverse and all living beings as being worthy of equal respect. Human beings are just one of the species on the planet, and as we are on the top of the pyramid, we have a lot of power. But instead of using and abusing this power, Jains believe we have the greatest responsibility and accountability to other living beings. These are the values on which I was raised, and as a result, I feel they have given me a huge reservoir of strength in contributing to our understanding and practice of diversity in British society. My culture has taught me to seek wisdom wherever it may lie, and respect others despite their size, status or origins. Every living being is worthy of the highest respect.

The sun never discriminates as to whom it shines its light on, so why should we? Jains take care not to harm even the smallest insects. We are all children of this vast planet, and there is room for us all. From a very young age, my family has taught me the highest level of integrity and humility. In fact, I have been taught to practise what I preach, so that my actions are synonymous with the things I write and say.

In truth, we are all different – no two people are exactly the same – we know this from our own families, let alone the outside world. It is a question of degree. Even we ourselves change over time and are different from one year to the next. Thus diversity is an individually experienced reality, not a choice or an issue. How we choose to accept it and live with it is what this book is about. The most important barrier to valuing and accepting diversity is the mind, and this is also the most important resource for change and transformation. Later in this book*, we will look at how we can cultivate and nourish open-mindedness.

## Learning from kids

Children are generally much more open-minded than adults. For very young children, diversity is no big issue; they just want to play or paint or create with whoever is around them. Provided their actions and judgements are not influenced by adults or the media, and they are exposed to different cultures, they can grow up quite broad-minded. I have made many friends from different backgrounds through my children. Their friendships encourage us to get to know one another. We recently had a dinner party at home with some English friends and our son reminded us quite casually that if it weren't for him, we wouldn't have made these new friends!

*Taken from Atul's book 'Celebrating Diversity'\**
*Published by Kevin Mayhew Ltd., Buxhall, Suffolk*

# Barbara Richardson-Todd:

# Losing God and finding Friends

I would like to share with you my personal journey of how I came to terms with losing God.

Rooted as a Roman Catholic in my early childhood, I spent the next forty or so years searching and exploring other flavours of Christianity, eastern religions, philosophies and ideologies, yet never finding the right fit for me. I have dipped into Buddhism (Zen, Tibetan and Western), Spiritualism, the ancient wisdoms, Wicca, Hinduism (Sri Chinmoy and Brahma Kumaris), the Mormons, and Headlessness with Douglas Harding, amongst others.

Along the way I met many wonderful and interesting people and could have stayed within their particular faith environment but for my realisation that this was not my belief and I could not go along with it or I would be hypocritical and disloyal to myself and my conscience.

A few years ago, through opportunistic meetings and following a TV programme that discussed the history of God or gods, things fell into place and I realised that, for me, there was no god. God was, like religion, a man-made construct developed to provide explanations for people in the days before science. Karen Armstrong, in 'A History of God', describes God as a "starter kit" from which we may be able to move on and evolve.

This revelation left me with a tremendous sense of loss. There was no protector or guardian angel to look after me and I had to take responsibility for my own life.

As well as a feeling of personal bereavement, there was a loss of the good things that religion can offer; the architecture of many beautiful buildings, the music, the joy of singing where no one cares what you sound like, the loss of praying (of talking and believing that someone listened and cared), traditions, weekly get-togethers, rituals, feasts, communal meals and celebrations. There is no comfort given on the loss of a loved one, no promise of heaven, as there is no belief in an afterlife. Most of all I missed a sense of community and of belonging; being with others who shared the same beliefs, ethics and actions.

I felt alone.

I agree with Alain de Botton in 'Religion for Atheists' who writes that we should learn from religion and take from it what is good, wise and beautiful and he even wrote new "commandments" or virtues for atheists. In the Bible, Philippians 4:8 concurs that "Whatever is true, whatever is honourable, whatever is just, whatever is pure, whatever is lovely, whatever is commendable, if there is any excellence, if there is anything worthy of praise, think about these things."

Books are informative, they provide evidence and help ease the feelings of not being the only one thinking along these lines but they don't cure the need for a community.

What was needed was a safe space for non-believers to meet and develop a new tradition and I found this through SIFRE of which I have been a part for more than twenty years. Even though my faith had been wavering, changing, evolving, I found comfort in conversing with others who had strong commitment or interest in religion and spirituality. An opportunistic encounter with the knowledgeable late Terence Cooper at a SIFRE meeting led to an exploration of several websites and forums.

Suddenly it all began to come together: I found the Sea of Faith Network and joined a lively, local group of wonderful, friendly, intelligent and funny people. In recent months, I have discovered the Quakers, The Religious Society of Friends, who are accepting and tolerant of anyone's viewpoint, whether theist or not, or anywhere in between on the spectrum. The Quakers have four main "testimonies" of truth and integrity, peace, equality and simplicity. The worship consists of sitting in silence for an hour with fellow "friends" and seeing that of God (whoever or whatever you consider this to be) in everyone. Within the Quaker organisation there are interest groups such as the Nontheist Network and the Universalists. It appears I am not alone in my thoughts and many more are now coming together to form communities of people who live a good life with virtuous beliefs but who are not religious in the main sense of the word.

I like Chris Stedman and his 'faitheism'* which calls for dialogue not division between the religious and the non-believer and bridging the gap between the angry atheists and religious pluralism in an interfaith world. He states that the "other" does not exist: we are in it together as a diverse humanity, respecting each one on our journey through life and the improvement of society. I totally agree with Stedman when he asks us to honour the unique humanity in everyone and he urges us "to step boldly and defiantly across dividing lines of religious and nonreligious identity and share our experiences in hope that we might build understanding through relationships of commitment and cooperation."

Atheists, nontheists, agnostics and non-believers are still able to appreciate the religions, faiths and views of others without sacrificing their own personal values and see each one is as valid as the other. It is healthy and right for non-religious people to be in conversation with the religious to identify areas of shared concern such as environmental issues, poverty, peace and so forth, and to work together for the good of all.

*Faitheist: How an Atheist Found Common Ground with the Religious

# Barry Spivack: Exploring my Jewish heritage

Orthodox Jews don't live in Suffolk. An orthodox Jew needs nine other Jews with whom he can pray, he needs to be able to walk to the house of prayer on the Sabbath and if he is not a vegetarian then he will want access to a kosher butcher. I moved to Suffolk at the end of 2006 and so one can gather that I am not an orthodox Jew. However I enjoy Jewish services and I enjoy mixing with other Jews.

Before moving to Suffolk I had been temporarily living in Brighton for ten months. Brighton has four synagogues, two orthodox, and is the only town in England with both a reform and a liberal community. The key theoretical distinction between orthodox Judaism and non-orthodox Judaism is that the orthodox believe that both the Torah and the oral law is the word of God, whereas the non-orthodox think that the Torah was inspired by God but written by man and the oral law was written by the Rabbis. Within the orthodox we can distinguish between the ultra-orthodox, whose black coats and hats are a leftover from eighteenth century eastern Europe, modern orthodox, who will keep all the commandments but otherwise cannot be identified by what they wear (although many will wear a yamulka on their head), and those who belong to an orthodox synagogue but may vary in how many commandments they actually obey.

Whilst in Brighton I visited all the different synagogues and they each had their own distinct feel and ethos. On moving to Suffolk I used Google to locate the nearest synagogue, which turned out to be in Colchester, an independent orthodox synagogue, fifty minutes' drive from where I live. There were also two synagogues in Norwich and Cambridge, one orthodox and one liberal in both cases. There was no synagogue in Suffolk. It seemed that Suffolk was a Judenfrei zone.

An orthodox Jew will pray three times a day. In most Jewish communities there will be services at least on Friday evenings, when the Sabbath commences, and on Saturday mornings and for the various Jewish holidays. The fifty-minute drive to Colchester was too far for the shorter Friday evening service and they rarely held services on a Saturday morning. This was a little frustrating.

A couple of years after moving to Suffolk I was looking at the national website for Liberal Judaism and by chance I noticed an email address for the Suffolk Jewish Community (SJC). I immediately followed this up and was delighted to find that four ladies who all belonged to the synagogue in Colchester but lived in Suffolk had started the SJC. At the time they held services on the last Friday of the month either in someone's home but more usually in hired premises.

On the first two occasions there were four or five of us. It is rare that more than fifteen attend a service. Our membership has just reached a record high by topping the thirty-member mark.

If any of us were devoted Jews we would not be living in Suffolk. But all of us feel a sense of belonging and familiarity which most but not all gained whilst growing up. It would be very difficult to generalise about our group as we all come to it in our own way with different needs and desires. I enjoy the prayers. Judaism is more about doing than believing but theology is obviously a central part of the religion. What one finds is that most Jews tend to focus on the bits of Judaism that appeal to them. It may be the emphasis on social justice or charity, or doing good deeds or it may be more inward and contemplative.

As a teenager I had no interest in Judaism. Having survived the ordeal of my barmitzvah I could forget all about it and just do enough to keep my parents satisfied. To me Judaism seemed only concerned with outer rituals and seemed superficial and repetitive. It seemed to lack any sort of genuine spirituality. I was interested in philosophy and social justice and I wasn't interested in having a set of beliefs. I wanted to know what was true. At university I studied Philosophy, Politics and Economics and whilst there I also learnt Transcendental Meditation, which involved no change in beliefs or lifestyle but simply gave the experience of inner silence. Whether it was a coincidence or not, I found that I made more of a connection with Judaism after I learnt

Transcendental Meditation. I found that the words of the prayers seemed more meaningful.

It was after the birth of my first son that I became more interested in Judaism and joined the Bedford Liberal Synagogue, and when I moved to St Albans I belonged to the Masorti synagogue (Masorti is between reform and orthodox) and when I lived in Regensburg in Bavaria for two years the only synagogue was orthodox, although a friend described it more accurately as non-observant orthodox as most of the congregation were relatively recent Russian immigrants who were Jewish in name rather than religious practice. One doesn't have to have a religion to teach one's children to be ethical and good citizens but I take the view that what has stood the test of time must have some value. With both of my sons I teach them about Judaism but I emphasise the ethical rather than ritual aspects although the ritual aspects are there to some extent. For example lighting candles on a Friday night and celebrating traditional Jewish festivals.

There is an old joke that a Jew on a desert island would build two synagogues as there has to be one he doesn't go to. I prefer towns where there is just one Jewish community – one size fits all. Then one can enjoy the diversity of how people relate to Judaism. Theologically I would describe myself as an agnostic who errs on the side of believing. I tend to take the view that most religions are describing the same thing but simply using a different language or vernacular and have developed different traditions and customs. I tend to look at what religions have in common and ignore the differences. On the other hand I would not consider going to a church or to a mosque to pray as that is not my tradition.

The prayers at the services remind me of both a deeper reality than one sees on the surface of life and one's responsibilities towards one's neighbours both near and far. I would prefer it if I had to travel less far for a service – it is generally a twenty-five minute drive. I would prefer it if we had services more often and more people attended. But I made a choice to live in Suffolk and implicit in that choice is that Jewish life would be sparse. My elder sister is orthodox and she lives in NW London where she has a large choice of synagogues of all denominations.

I am currently on the committee of the SJC. It is possible that as the university in Suffolk develops we may attract more Jewish students and members of faculty. I am proud of my Jewish heritage but over time the essence and inner meaning of religion can get lost, which is why I also enjoy my practice of Transcendental Meditation and the two give me both a sense of spiritual development and fulfilment.

# Betty Wells: Who is not my neighbour?

I am a country girl at heart, brought up in a small Norfolk village and currently living in Mellis, on the Norfolk-Suffolk border. I was baptised as a baby into the Church of England but as a child I attended the local Methodist Sunday School. It was within safe walking distance whereas the local Anglican Church was a few miles away. I was not confirmed until I was sixteen and thereafter my attendance at church services went in fits and starts, not becoming regular until we moved here to Mellis.

Having trained as a teacher, I worked in schools in various places in the UK. We eventually settled in Mellis in 1983 and have remained here ever since. We arrived on 22nd December and our first introduction to Mellis Church was the Midnight Mass on Christmas Eve.

It was not long before I was asked to join the Parochial Church Council and later to represent Mellis Church on the local Synod of the Deanery of Hartismere. I am now also a Churchwarden at Mellis and am the Lay-Chair of Hartismere Deanery Synod. There is usually not much competition for these posts!

Mellis is an attractive village as it is blessed with a large common, one of the largest in Suffolk. The two owners, or Lords of the Manor, are the Suffolk Wildlife Trust and a private individual. This wonderful grazing common is renowned for its wild flowers, particularly orchids, and attracts the attention of those who enjoy the countryside. It is understandably a favourite stopping place for the travelling community, especially for those with horses to graze, and different groups have visited over the years.

I was thrilled to bits the first time I saw that people with two bow-topped waggons had stopped there. These first temporary neighbours were new age travellers and, although I felt a deep connection with them immediately and eventually made friends with them, my attitude was not shared by everyone in the village and a lot of tension was caused by their presence. I don't understand why I felt so comfortable with them but the feeling was so strong that it made me wonder if I have any Gypsy ancestors, although I'm not aware of any. I do know, however, how much I have appreciated meeting most of those who have stayed over the years, including Irish travellers and Romany families as well as various new age travellers.

In a small village it can be very painful when there is dissent. Some of the ill will expressed by a few of our fellow villagers was based on bad experiences but much of it was blind prejudice. On the rare occasions when trash was left behind, the village bore the cost of clearing up. This made it difficult for traveller families who did behave well while here and for those of us who supported them.

I have on one occasion been asked to lock the church when there were travellers in the area but I did not feel this was the right response. Fortunately both our parish clergy and our local police have been open-minded and wise in their dealings with these guests of ours.

The police have been able to allay fears about those travellers who will not cause trouble and the clergy have been prepared to extend pastoral care when needed. On one occasion we were privileged to hold a baptism actually on the common for a Gypsy baby and I am particularly privileged to be her Godmother. We brought the Paschal Candle from the church and used a mini Gypsy jack for the water. When the family moved on I lost contact for a while but I am glad to say that I am now back in touch with my little god-daughter, Louanna, and her family, and we exchange presents at Christmas. So these temporary neighbours of mine have brought me much pleasure and I have learnt a lot from them about their way of life. I am also the proud owner of my own traditional Gypsy bow-topped waggon!

I have also been on a steep learning curve as a result of various visits to the Holy Land, beginning in 2006. Initially we went on a Christian tour which was followed by courses at St George's College in Jerusalem and then by an independent arrangement which included a 4-day Green Olive tour during which we stayed with a Christian Palestinian family in Bethlehem. Since then we have been twice more, culminating this year with a conference in Bethlehem called Christ at the Checkpoint. As we actually stayed in Bethlehem we saw first-hand some of the horrors and humiliations suffered daily by innocent civilians including children. We have been amazed by the courage of the people we met and of their perseverance in trying to make a living and survive. Most pilgrims or tourists see only the Church of the Nativity, buy souvenirs and are then bussed quickly out again. They may barely notice the checkpoint or the Wall or the powerful messages painted on walls by the artist Banksy and by other people who have visited, looked about them and been outraged by what they saw there.

There are many times in the gospels when Jesus urges his

contemporaries, especially the leaders, to open their eyes and not to remain in the dark and he called peacemakers "Children of God". His message is still relevant today. Our eyes need to be open to what is happening to our neighbours, to those like the travelling community, who are marginalised in our own country, and those further away, like the peoples of the Middle East. We need to work for peace, wherever we can. But it is hard not to despair.

My Vicar gave me this prayer a while ago, when I was feeling particularly beleaguered trying to stand up for a Gypsy encampment in the village, and I found it has given me comfort and strength, both then and since.

*Deep peace of the running wave to you.*
*Deep peace of the flowing air to you.*
*Deep peace of the quiet earth to you.*
*Deep peace of the shining stars to you.*
*Deep peace of the gentle night to you.*
*Moon and stars pour their healing light on you.*
*Deep peace of Christ,*
*Of Christ the light of the world to you.*
*Deep peace of Christ to you.*

# Beverley Levy: The Jewish way of life

Jewish teachings revolve around questions of ethics, of man's treatment of his fellow man (or woman). There are some expressions that capture this sense of treating one's neighbours and community with compassion and fairness, such as "Do not do unto others what you would not have done to yourself" and then again, "Thou shalt love thy neighbour as thyself", which is from Leviticus 19:18. Jewish people are commanded to help those in need, both physical and financial and to help both Jews and strangers.

I was brought up amongst a very traditional Jewish family and like all families my parents were very busy simply making a living and getting through the week. They were not learned and teachings were transmitted via example, in the way that they were. I now have a few wonderful books handed down to me by my parents that are actually about the teachings and in one book it explains what the Talmud says about community. The Talmud is the writings that give guidance on how to live. In this book 'Everyman's Talmud' I read:

"Man is not intended to live alone but as a member of society. He is a unit in the body of humanity... His life is not his own to do with as he pleased. His conduct affects his neighbours as their conduct affects him."

There are further teachings that stress the importance of being independent – "If I am not for myself, who will be for me? And being for myself, what am I?" – but that this shouldn't be carried too far. In Jewish teachings it is believed that an isolated life is not worth living and that it is desirable to seek co-operation and mutual assistance; "If you will lift the load I will lift too, but if you will not lift it, I will not."

We hope that Jewish people are a valued part of the social landscape. This year celebrates 350 years since the Jews returned to Britain, in 1656, after being expelled in 1290 by Edward I. There have never been many Jewish people living in Ipswich, and the last synagogue was demolished in 1877 after it had fallen into disrepair. It is now possible for local Jewish people to meet and celebrate the festivals. We are doing this in the style of Liberal Judaism which attempts to bring ancient teachings in line with contemporary life, accepting that most of us lead secular lives completely assimilated, with the people we live amongst.

By celebrating festivals that are couched in our own ancient mythology we are able to confirm our identity. By association I would consider that a healthy society is one in which people from different ethnic backgrounds are able to securely celebrate their own mythologies and commonalities; an even healthier society is one in which we are not only tolerant of each other's cultures, but join in. One year we had a Holocaust Memorial Service on 27th January in the synagogue in Colchester that was attended by people from different local churches.

On that same weekend the Chinese community were celebrating their New Year of the Lazy Dog on 28th January and we were invited to join in with the celebrations. It helps to make us all feel included in that thing called community.

# Bhupinder Sually: My particular Sikh path

There are various Sikh paths or sects reflecting the different historical and social contexts in which the faith was born and has developed. In particular the caste system has had a lasting influence, and the 10th Guru, Gobind Singh, sought to overcome this when he formed the Khalsa (collected body of all initiated Sikhs).

All but one believe that the Guru Granth Sahib is the 10th and Final Guru.

I belong to the Radha Soami faith, which believes that the teachings of All Saints are universal, and can lead us back to our origin. We use the teachings of the holy Granth to express our faith and guide our path, while also believing in a Living Guru or Spiritual Guide. This belief is confirmed by the teachings contained in the Guru Granth Sahib, which includes the teachings of 22 other saints, both Hindu and Muslim holy people, as well as the 10 Sikh Gurus. Our national spiritual centre is at Haynes Park, Bedford. Haynes Park is owned by the sangat and sewa (service) on this huge farm takes place every day and most devotees go there over the weekend. In particular, the sangat (congregation) meets for two discourses over several days annually in May and August. Often the Master is present.

There are four criteria to being accepted as a disciple of the Masters:
Complete vegetarianism; no meat, no fish, no eggs.
No alcohol or drugs.

These first two are absolute obligations. In addition we aspire to keep the moral promise of one husband and one wife (and no sex before marriage).

The observation of 2½ hours of meditation daily (between 3 and 6 am, a tenth of a day) and we are asked to give what we can of our income in charity.

# Charles Croydon: Living as an Anglican

As a personal introduction, I was born in Ipswich on the north side of Christchurch Park. I have two older sisters. Four months after I was born I was christened in the Ipswich Anglican Church of St Mary-le-Tower.

Among my dominant early memories was that as a family we attended St Mary-le-Tower. In the blue carpeted children's corner of St Mary-le-Tower I was read Bible stories and taught a shortened version of Sir Richard of Chichester's prayer, "Dear Lord Jesus, redeemer, friend and brother, may I know thee more clearly, love thee more dearly, follow thee more nearly, day by day. Amen." At that time I did not know what a redeemer was. My mother prayed with me every evening.

My first head teacher, Miss Fryer, worshipped at St Mary-le-Tower. I cried on the music stool on my first day at school. My next head teacher, Miss Ransome, also worshipped at this church. So my early influences were of being steeped in the culture of St Mary-le-Tower, which, then as now, had a strong choral tradition. I continued in Christian schools initially with one service of worship a day and an occasional Sunday service of worship at school which then changed to two services of worship a day and every Sunday a service of worship at school. At the age of fourteen I was confirmed at school.

Then there was rock and roll. The Isle of Wight pop festival (our British version of Woodstock), Jimmy Hendrix's last concert on the Isle of Wight, The Who, and waking up to John Sebastian's dulcet tones.

At college my liberal education was challenged. I remember being asked what sort of communist I was, whether a right wing speaker be allowed a platform to speak, and if professional qualification should be withheld if students went on strike. Maggie Thatcher was rising to power. My attendance at worship rather fell by the wayside.

After college my first home was in Manhattan, which I found noisy after the tranquillity of Suffolk. I lived opposite The General Theological Seminary and it was through visiting this Episcopalian Seminary to find some escape from the hustle and bustle of business life that my religious life was reawakened. This came with challenges as in visiting there I became aware of issues such as apartheid in South Africa and I remember being asked who I thought should pay for a black lesbian to become a priest; to put this in context at that time in Atlanta, Georgia, there was clearly a Woolworths for 'blacks' and a Woolworths for 'whites'.

In terms of later developments, at 27 I was back in Ipswich, married, and spent the next 15 years worshipping at the Ipswich Anglican Church of St John the Baptist. Three children were born, were christened and went to Church of England voluntary aided primary schools.

Post modernism arrived; technology was not just about someone from the USA walking on the moon but great choice. In the 1960s there were about five pirate radio stations one could listen to. In the 1990s there were more than five thousand on the internet.

My experience of mortality changed. No longer was I protected from the death of a grandparent, but I was now responding directly to the death of close family members. Priorities changed abruptly. Grieving became part of my personal life.

From the age of 32 I became a Tearfund church representative and then became involved in local One World Week activities. Later on I supported the Anglican Diocesan World Development Adviser. I remember going to Anglican Diocesan World Development meetings and discussing on the journey if where we were born would result in us having a different faith.

I became active with the Ipswich and District One World Centre and Christian Aid. The Ipswich and District One World Centre merged with the Ipswich and District United Nations Association. I began to be involved with Inter-faith activities through my involvement with the

Anglican Diocesan World Development Adviser and after the age of thirty-nine I became involved with the Ipswich and District United Nations Association Interfaith Celebration of Human Rights. So began my involvement with SIFRE.

At the age of 40 I remarried, moved, and changed to worshipping at the local Ipswich Anglican Church of St Margaret's, where I still am. I became increasingly involved in social issues such as Christian Aid and the Ipswich Soup Kitchen. In particular I supported the Anglican Diocesan Environmental Adviser on climate change issues. Recently I have been in involved with Suffolk Churches for Zimbabwe, raising awareness of the situation in Zimbabwe and raising funds for Tearfund projects there.

To be a Christian – in my heart being a Christian means being moved by compassion and to show that love in action as best I can. In practice being Christian means involvement in the voluntary sector. I currently chair the Ipswich and District United Nations Association. Today the United Nations will feed 900 million people. I lead on organising, with help from SIFRE, the annual United Nations Association Inter-faith Celebration of Human Rights. I lead one of the Thursday evening soup kitchen teams, I am St Margaret's Church Representative for Christian Aid, and last year helped to raise funds for 3:1 match funding from the European Union for a maternal health project in eastern Sierra Leone. I am currently organising a quiz to raise funds for 3:1 match funding from the European Union for a literacy project for women in Afghanistan. I lead the St Margaret's Environment Group, I am a member of St Margaret's Interfaith Outreach Group which has twice organised the playing of the Diversity Game (with support from SIFRE). Last year we had an exchange visit with the Ipswich Sikhs and recently organised a visit to the Unitarian Meeting House for their Flower Communion. I have also helped organise an evening of Celtic Christianity and film show as part of our Church Outreach.

There have been many special events in my life to reflect on. I have had a fortunate life with family and friends to love and be loved by. So far I have had good health and material prosperity, and I have lived through a time of European peace. I consider that not only do we have to treat others as we would want to be treated, but loving our neighbour means global not local. Climate change affects the poorest most, so how I use energy will affect farmers in Africa. I also need to learn from them how to shrink my carbon footprint.

I also feel a need to learn forgiveness from others and to try to pass that on. So, for example, I am promoting a booklet written by 'The Forgiveness Project' containing real stories of crime and violence in order to explore how ideas around forgiveness, reconciliation and conflict resolution can be used to impact positively on people's lives. Their personal testimonies and portraits provide insight and inspiration and these narratives of hope seem to tap into a deep public need for alternative and peaceful responses to hurt and violence.

At the age of 61 I went with the Anglican Diocesan Pilgrimage to the Holy Land with Bishop Nigel Stock and found only one site where a church had not been built; a bay on the north west corner of the Sea of Galilee which forms a natural amphitheatre. Peter Walker in his book 'In the Steps of Jesus' says to the west of "Capernaum there is a small bay that has been demonstrated to act as a natural amphitheatre. Mark tells us that, on at least one occasion, the crowd gathered round Jesus was 'so large that he got into a boat and sat in it out on the lake', while all the people were along the shore at the water's edge (Mark 4:11). This small bay, the acoustic 'centre' of which is less than 10 feet from the shore could have been the ideal spot. It is not hard to imagine people hanging onto Jesus' every word as the quiet water lapped the boat." This bay is known as 'Sower's Bay' after the parable of the sower. The lapping sound of the Sea of Galilee reminded me of the sound of water I had heard elsewhere as I have sailed all my life.

In 2012 I visited the Mauer Museum by what was Checkpoint Charlie in Berlin. I learnt about the Berlin Wall but l left feeling it was historic, something of the past, different to when I visited the Anne Frank House in Amsterdam, where at the end of the tour current human rights issues are presented to the visitor.

While I had heard of Winston Churchill's speech about an "iron curtain descending over Europe from Stettin in the Baltic to Trieste in the Adriatic", I did not know until recently that two years after this speech, the final touches would be made to a plan for the systematic expulsion of the Palestinians from vast areas of their country. I also did not know that two years after the Berlin Wall was torn down the then prime minister of Israel, Yitzhak Rabin, was proposing that a new wall be built; a physical barrier between the Israeli and Palestinian populations. I now think I was naive to consider the Berlin Wall was part of the past and there would be no more walls. I should have known better. I remember now Roger Water's lyric of "… you are just another brick in the wall …" from Pink Floyd's album 'The Wall', and Gerald Scarfe's cartoon of animated marching hammers in the film version of 'The Wall'.

As I write this piece, in my heart, I am angry about the unholy mess the Israeli government is making of the Holy Land. Being a Christian I feel called to not only speak out, but to learn about the historical background and support those involved in peace making and helping in a humanitarian way, and then I cry.

On the Anglican Diocesan Pilgrimage to the Holy Land we only saw part of the 750 km long wall/barrier. Some local people had made their mark on some parts of the bleak concrete. While we can pray for the peace of Jerusalem, it strikes me that God is active in the worst situations. This was reflected in the people we met and what they do. On this pilgrimage I was moved by the plight of the Palestinians, the work of the Holy Family Hospital and International Centre in Bethlehem. However I was most touched by the talk by Bassam and Rami, a Palestinian and an Israeli, who were once dedicated fighters willing to kill and be killed by one another for the sake of their nations. Yet each one of them came face to face with the price of war when their daughters were killed in the conflict. Left with the excruciating pain of bereavement, they chose to do the unexpected. They set out on a joint journey to humanise the very enemy, which had taken from their dearest and beloved daughters and to prevent the vicious cycle of retaliation in themselves and their societies. At the end of their talk Bassam said to me it is a matter of "The Love of Power and the Power of Love."

We are fortunate in Suffolk that there are many initiatives helping to bring communities together, such as Ipswich being a 'Town of Sanctuary'. SIFRE is one of these that, in my view, works to humanise, remove walls and barriers, and help to understand the "Power of love."

# Chinmayi Nath:
## Inspired by my Hindu background

I came to England with my husband in 2003. My son is 7 years old and I have completed more than 9 years in Ipswich. My native place is Odisha, in the eastern part of India. Being from India, I am glad to be associated with the vast richness of Hindu culture and the elusive beauty of its spiritual tradition. It is a most ancient religion which teaches us basic values of life that sustain us and has given immense wisdom, a glorious culture and rich traditions to uphold life and build a better society.

Being from Odisha, an eastern state of India, we traditionally follow Lord Jagannath, along with his brother Balabhadra and his sister Subhadra. Jagannath is considered as an incarnation of Vishnu and also as a form of Buddha as well as a manifestation of Krishna. The colour of the deities – Jagannatha (black), Balabhadra (white) and Subhadra (yellow) – possibly represent the skin colour combinations of all the people of the world and helps to spread the maxim of universal brotherhood. The idol of Jagannath is made of special neem wood with large round eyes, with stumps as hands and with no legs, which is the representation of Brahman as close as possible, because he symbolises the formlessness of God who is the foremost, the great infinite being. The temple of Jagannath in Puri is recognised as one of the sacred Hindu pilgrimage places in India. Jagannath is also known as Patita Pavana, which signifies all the merciful aspects of God.

Jagannath, Balabhadra and Subhadra come outside of the temple during Rath Yatra (Chariot festival), allowing the public to have a holy view. The most significant ritual associated with the Chariot festival is the chhera pahara, when the Gajapati King, the King of Odisha, sweeps all around the deities and chariots. This ritual signifies that under the lordship of Jagannath there is no distinction between the powerful sovereign king and the most humble devotee. I always admire these aspects associated with our tradition and culture.

I am an artist and my passion for Indian Art has also supported me to know more about my culture and religion. I have observed that our ancient Indian art was not just to adorn the walls but to narrate a story and most of the Hindu artworks are illustrated scenes from epics like Ramayan and Mahabharat and other mythological stories which continue to inspire artists even now. These artefacts have helped in strengthening our cultural values and preserving heritage and history.

I have always been fascinated by the Patachitra art of Odisha, an ancient religious Indian art which originated from a small village, Raghurajpur, near Puri, which goes back to the 8th century AD. Patachitra art is performed on cloth using natural colour which can be traced back to the establishment of the shrine of Lord Jagannath at Puri in Odisha. The subject matter of the patachitras includes religious, mythological, and folk themes based on Krishna Leela and Lord Jagannath. It has inspired me to work on patachitra paintings and also helped me to make a small documentary on this folk art and its artists using digital media during my research project on contemporary art and design study in the UK. Our religion and culture has always inspired me to get attached to the core of native themes of India and is also reflected in my artwork in this modern era.

Since my childhood, my parents taught us to believe in God, the supreme power. It makes you strong and helps you to believe in your own strength and guides you in the right path of life. As a Hindu, I always believe in and respect other religions. Hinduism explains God is the same in every religion but is worshipped in different ways by different names in different times.

Hindu scriptures, however, have not given any definition of Hinduism. It is in fact not the name of a religion but the "way of life" of the people inhabiting the land of Sindhu. It is better to replace Hindu religion by Sanatana Dharma. It is a way of life which has been enhanced by various learned persons, philosophers and great followers of God through time and space. The moral values we perceive from these our ancestors play an important role in our life.

I am very fortunate to have received a few years of my initial education from the Sri Aurobindo School in Cuttack, Odisha. Aurobindo was a great freedom fighter, philosopher, poet and also a spiritual leader. He founded the Sri Aurobindo Ashram, in Pondicherry along with the help of his spiritual collaborator, Mirra Alfassa (The Mother). He dedicated his life to serve humanity in the areas of education, medical services and social services among the poor and needy. I remember how those school days started with a meditation around the Samadhi and after that we were allowed to visit Sri Aurobindo's and the Mother's room. Meditation helps to develop deep focus in your work and gives calmness of mind. The history of meditation is intimately bound up with the religious context. Since prehistoric times, civilisations in India used repetitive, rhythmic chants and offerings to appease the gods. I used to visit my school in Odisha during my return visits to India.

I would like to share a few childhood memories of time spent with my late grandpa. He was a humble English teacher, a voracious reader and also a great admirer of Gandhiji, the Father of the nation, India. He used to give us small storybooks related to moral values and also related to Vivekanand and Mahatma Gandhi's ideology as and when we met him. My grandpa also advised us to follow Gandhiji's point of view regarding the true religious and social ideas of Hinduism. Gandhiji has taught people the value of nonviolence, truth, the welfare of all without exclusion and service to mankind. Our religion believes in the Law of Karma. It states that, any action that we do in life has some 'Fruit' or 'Consequence' attached to it. Our religion always teaches us about worship, that the work you do is the true means of worshipping God and that the best way of using your knowledge and education is to use them in the service of mankind.

Hinduism represents a very broad and diverse philosophy embedded within the religion. One of its philosophical tenets is to give respect to parents, teachers, and elders. We touch our elders' feet to greet them, which is a sign of respect and a humble way of acknowledging their love to us. I remember one Sloka on this which I learnt from childhood time.

"Gurur Brahma Gurur Vishnuhu Guru Devo Maheswaraha Guru Saakshaat Parabhrahma Tasmai Sri Gurave Namaha".

The true meaning of Guru is one who disperses the darkness of ignorance. In Hinduism the Supreme Guru is Lord Brahma, alongside Vishnu and Maheswara. They are the creator, preserver and transformer of knowledge respectively. We respect teachers as Gurus as they help us to gain knowledge. Hinduism also explains that mother and father are your first Gurus as they bring you to this beautiful world and they give you the first lessons of life. So we always prostrate before them to get their blessings.

In our religion, knowledge is the greatest of all forms of wealth. It always guides your actions and thoughts in the right way. We always worship Lord Ganesha and Goddess Saraswati during morning prayer as they are the God and Goddess of knowledge, wisdom, intelligence, success and prosperity in Hinduism. Our religion also teaches us to live together in a family. There are many examples of this present in the Hindu Epics – Ramayan and Mahabharat. This tradition of strong family ties has made it distinct from western culture.

I have been working in different community centres for local people in Ipswich. These beliefs have always helped me to carry out my work in the right way. At the moment, I am working at Ipswich Hindu Samaj Community Centre and Mandir to organise various youth and children's activities. Associating with this organisation helps me to know more about our religious beliefs and to share these good values to the youth and children of our community through different activities, like organising religious and cultural events, informing them about the mythological and moral stories in our culture, teaching them to chant mantras and Vedic prayers and also providing meditation and yoga. We are able to provide these good ethics of Hinduism to our children in the UK through this organisation.

Hinduism teaches selflessness and sacrifice, respecting elders, staying together in a family, emphasising one's responsibilities rather than rights, self-discipline and simplicity of life-style. These values have moulded not only my education but also my life, taught me how to live and how to become a true being.

I am trying my best to share these good values in the upbringing of my son while I am staying in the United Kingdom and also to convey them to the people of our community to the best of my ability.

# Dali Jabbar: A Parsee on the railways

I was born in Mombasa, Kenya, in 1941 but moved to the UK at the age of nineteen, hoping to find an apprenticeship in engineering. Although I came by myself I was not unduly apprehensive as Kenya was a British colony and so I was not expecting too much of a culture shock. A few things did surprise me, though, including how few people had cars, how difficult it was to get lodgings in Peterborough and, even worse, my failure to secure an apprenticeship as the training was 5 years and I was considered too old. My second choice was farming but again I was unable to get a placement. And so I joined the railways. After an eight-week course I became a telegraph lad, assisting the signalman, with responsibility to send single needle telegrams. I also had to clean the signal box, clear out the ashes from the coal fire and refill the coal bucket. In 1962, aged 20, after another 8 weeks training, I became the only Asian to pass as a signalman.

For the first few years as a single man I shared a room in a two-bedroomed house with another man, each of us paying £1 per week. After a while a Gujurati Patel family moved into the house and took me under their wing. But eventually I felt it was time to find a wife and returned to Kenya in 1967 with that in mind. I also went to India on the same quest. I should say at this point that I could not marry any girl who took my fancy as my family was Zoroastrian (or Parsee as known in India) and I could not marry out. Family members would usually take some responsibility for introducing their young people to suitable partners and that is what I was expecting to happen. However, in 1970 I had the good fortune to catch sight of the young girl who is now my wife when she was out for a walk. I was able to get an introduction to her as she was also a Parsee. I continued to work in Peterborough and our daughter was born there.

In 1981 we moved to Ipswich so that I could take up a higher-grade signalman's post and I spent many years working shifts, including weekends, while also becoming involved in union work and in local politics. In 1985 I also became a magistrate which helped to develop the diversity of the bench. Between 1990 and 2007, as a member of Ipswich Borough Council, I served on various committees, including development control. By this time I felt totally integrated into the local community, but I was not connected to any local religious group. As a Zoroastrian I was in a very tiny minority group in the UK and so when I lived in Peterborough we maintained a connection with the faith of our family by going to London twice a year and I have continued to do this. The special times of the year in my tradition are in the spring at the Festival of No Ruz and in September when we honour our dead, when the community gathers at Brookwood Cemetery in Surrey.

From childhood I have tried to live an ethical life and to be of service to my local community. There are three Zoroastrian precepts which have helped me to focus on this. They are:

MANASHNI ****** GOOD THOUGHTS
GAVASHNI ****** GOOD WORDS
KUNASHNI ****** GOOD DEEDS

I retired from the railways at the end of 2006 and from the magistracy at the end of 2011.

# Dawn Crisp: A Baptist in rural Suffolk

I was born and brought up in rural Suffolk into a largely Baptist family. As my dad worked away my early years were spent predominantly with my mum and because of this, church prayer meetings often took place in our home so I had an early introduction to the love and fellowship that comes from a place of prayer. I also remember my grandparents specifically praying for me when I started high school that I would have a circle of Christian friends there. And so I did …

Whilst at school we were blessed with Christian members of staff who took their time to encourage us at school. We went to Mission England (Billy Graham's Crusade) in 1984 in Ipswich, as well as concerts and youth celebrations all around Suffolk.

However, by the age of 17 I had begun to appreciate that the Bible actually teaches that our belief in Jesus is a personal faith, not an inherited way of life. As such, this was now my journey and the faith my parents and grandparents had demonstrated and shared with me – although an influence – was not my ticket to heaven!

After leaving high school and starting work, in order to keep in touch with my friends from school we all met up at a Baptist Church youth club once a week. We then started attending Sunday services together and gradually one by one felt God speak to each of us. Being part of a growing youth group where for the first time I was surrounded by young people, for whom this Christianity had not necessarily been their upbringing, was new for me. They were keen to understand more about the Bible and what God wanted for them. Witnessing a baptism service one Sunday evening in Occold, and hearing the speaker talk about Jesus healing Bartimaeus of his blindness, I understood for the first time that although I could see physically, I needed Jesus to heal me of my spiritual blindness and open my eyes to all that He could do for me too. On that night I sensed an overwhelming sense of peace as I recognised for the first time that the Bible I had been brought up to believe was actually real and true – and could be relevant to me.

I remember that at that point in time, I did not understand it all but that I needed to place my trust in Jesus. The next few years were not an easy time. I lost my mum to cancer and experienced loss for the first time. But knowing she had true faith and was able to look forward to a new life in heaven, without any more pain was, and still is, a huge comfort.

God has given me a wonderful husband who also became a Christian as a teenager. Over the past 20 years we have both been involved in working with young people in our local church – sharing the good news about Jesus that our youth leaders shared with us – even more important in these days when so many have not even heard of Jesus and what he can mean to them. We have also tried to get involved in community life in order to demonstrate that being a Christian does not make us weird – but actually people who can be relied upon – just as we rely on Jesus. So we help at village events when we can, trying to get to know people. We hope and pray that in getting to know us, and other friends in our local church, those around us will see Jesus and want to know Him too.

# Denis Johnston: Finding my way to Humanism

I grew up in fairly religious environment. I nearly wrote "religious household", but that would not be accurate. My parents were regular churchgoers but at home religion played little part in day-to-day life. Unlike many around us, my parents didn't say grace at meals, didn't "God bless" people and didn't say peculiar things like "d-v" at the end of every sentence when making plans.

To explain further; I was brought up in Belfast in Northern Ireland. This was in the 1950s and although it was a time of relative peace compared to before and what was to come later, it was still a time of sectarian tension.

I suppose I first became aware that our family was a little different from many around us when I was at primary school. The difference was that although we were Protestants, my dad was not an Orangeman.

For those unfamiliar with Northern Irish politics, the Orange order is a quasi-religious-political organisation. Its declared main purpose is to defend protestant civil and religious liberties and the various unionist political parties were closely allied to it. The popular slogan, "A Protestant Parliament for a Protestant People," pretty well summed it up.

Many of our neighbours and a few relatives on my father's side were Orangemen. My great-grandfather's orange and purple sash, alongside some bits of Masonic regalia, was stored in a cardboard box on the top of the wardrobe in my bedroom.

Come the twelfth of July, when the Orangemen complete with banners, drums and pipes would march through the centre of Belfast, my father would have none of it. So while most of my friends were taken by their fathers and uncles to the big event at "the field" that was the culmination of their march, I was at home. At "the field" the Orangemen would be regaled by politicians, ministers and Orange Lodge officials. There they would celebrate the glorious historical victory of Protestantism over Catholicism in 1690 and renew their pledge to keep it that way.

Some of my father's scepticism may have come from my mother's side of the family, the Boyds. They were not religious at all. Bohemian might be a more appropriate term. My great uncle Tommy was an ardent trade unionist, my great-great Aunt Ida had stood as a Labour candidate (a totally futile gesture) and claimed to be the first woman in N Ireland to have ridden a motorcycle. This side of the family was steeped in Irish politics, history and the arts. One uncle had smuggled a first-edition copy of James Joyce's 'Ulysses' from Paris into Ireland where it was a proscribed book. In a notable reversal of fortunes, that same volume is now in a centrepiece glass case in the Linenhall Library in the centre of the city.

My parents had met at a "wee dance" held in a scout hall in the east of the city. My father had been an enthusiastic member of the scouts – a member of one of the few open scout troops in N Ireland. Open scout troops were those not affiliated to any church and were something of a rarity. As a consequence, his scout group contained both Roman Catholics and Protestants of all flavours. The scout hall was adjacent to the notorious Short Strand area of East Belfast, which was at that time a small, predominately Roman Catholic enclave. Bounded on one side by the river Lagan but otherwise just inside the large area of staunchly protestant working class East Belfast, it was one of the sectarian flashpoint areas of the city.

As a child I was unaware of the backgrounds of the two sides of the family but I was aware that there were often debates about "important things", especially on Sunday afternoons. That was because we got our first television in the middle of the 1950s and on Sunday afternoons there was a programme called 'The Brains Trust'. Although, initially, there was a "No TV on Sunday" rule, it didn't apply to this programme. On a Sunday afternoon we would have a full house. Relatives (mainly but not exclusively from my mother's side) would gather to watch this. I, of course, was, "shooshed" out of the room but I can still remember the excitement and arguments and discussions of the adults that followed. Looking back I can see why. The Brains Trust asked viewers to send in difficult questions for the panellists on moral, ethical and political issues.

I see now that reports of the time claimed "that it appeared that the typical intellectual appearing on the Brains Trust was likely to be both agnostic and socialist" and that "it had managed to upset both the government and the church."

Of course I had no grasp of the issues discussed but I can still visualise the images of those philosophers on the tiny black and white screen of almost sixty years ago. I think something must have stuck.

Education: Most children at my primary school came from the skilled working class families with parents who worked in the shipyard, the aircraft factory and the brand new synthetic fibre companies.

These were parents who were generally upwardly mobile and were ambitious. For them, Harding Memorial Primary School was just the place. It taught the three Rs (plus a fourth, religious instruction) relentlessly and to the total exclusion of everything else and it had correspondingly good academic results. At the age of eleven we all had to sit what was known as the "Qually" – the secondary school qualifying examination and the precursor to what later became the 11-plus. Passing this meant that you could go to grammar school, failing it meant the secondary modern. Harding's 75% success rate was seven times the national average.

It was a tough school for ten and eleven-year-olds. As the "Qually" approached, we were caned for every sum we got wrong in our weekly tests. Fear of the cane was only matched by fear of failing to get into a grammar school.

The approach to religious instruction (RI) was equally rigorous and the first lesson of the day was always RI. Most children were from families with Presbyterian or Church of Ireland traditions and much of the teaching was rote learning of verses. There were also catechisms, creeds and even prayer responses. None of this made any sense to me as the Congregational church my parents attended had no truck with such things. I can remember querying this with my mother and her saying, "If they ask you, just say you are a Congregationalist." It was like a magic word!

Every year, always on a Thursday morning in early spring, the annual RI inspection took place. A minister would appear in class and I can recall classmates being required to recite things. I was never included (probably deliberately), to my considerable relief. The great thing about the RI inspection was that if the class did well, which it always did, then we got the rest of the day off. So it wasn't all bad.

I also went to Sunday school but never liked it. It was the most boring hour of the week -- colouring in, happy-clappy songs, one boring (or even frightening) Bible story after another and more rote learning of verses. However apart from canings and Sunday school I had a very happy childhood and although I now realise that my parents were not at all well off, I always felt that I had a very privileged life.

I passed the "Qually" and I also passed a special entrance exam for one of Belfast's better independent grammar schools. Moving to a secondary school is daunting for all youngsters and so I found it. However, the most alarming discovery was that most of the other boys in my class (it was an all-boys school of course) were of a different background. Sons of professionals (and politicians), they had a confidence that I had never seen before. Some had even been abroad. I can recall one teacher pointing at three of us in the class and saying, "You three – you all went to Harding — your spelling is perfect, your arithmetic is perfect but none of you have a clue who is the prime minister." Our primary education had been focussed on the three Rs to exclusion of everything else, and it clearly showed.

At this school we had "Divinity" instead of RI. The first couple of years were little more than an extension of primary school but in the third year this changed and we started "Comparative Religion". From the Ziggurats of Ur, the Yin and Yang of Taoism, Zoroastrianism, through Hinduism, Buddhism and Judaism, and a few other -isms on the way, we learned of the origins and practices of today's main beliefs.

The great thing about Divinity classes was that there were no examinations. We discussed, we talked and we learnt. And as we progressed, it moved from religion to philosophy and ethics. Words like existentialism were bandied about. Names such as Kant, Kierkegaard and Wittgenstein were sprinkled around. Ideas of logic, e.g. the impossibility of proving a negative, were covered and were explained. Although I didn't grasp much of it, some of the ideas of ethical and critical thinking were probably seeded there.

I also remember learning of an organisation called Voluntary Service Overseas (VSO). Whatever it was I thought that it sounded pretty special.

At school I loved the science and mathematics; I was a nerd well before the term was invented and it was pretty inevitable that I would end up studying engineering at university. Just before I started my degree course I was also offered one of three undergraduate apprenticeships awarded every year by the local aircraft factory. This meant that the theory taught at university was complemented with a vast array of shop floor and craft skills. However I had a problem. At the end of my apprenticeship I ended up in the most advanced (and interesting) part of the organisation. This was the dynamics division. In aerospace, dynamics is a euphemism for guided missiles, and I was not comfortable with working in the arms industry. I also realised by this time that I had become an atheist. It was not something that happened overnight, just a gradual realisation that the religious beliefs I had been brought up with, and which I now realise were pretty fundamentalist, no longer made sense. Moreover, by this time the sectarian conflict in N Ireland had worsened and despite the protestations of many that it was nothing to do with religion that just didn't ring true.

Another factor was that I was by then working in the aircraft factory where the production line was in full production. I was in the R & D division by then but would also be on the shop floor. Here those assembling the missiles would regularly sing hymns and psalms as they worked. It was bizarre for they were fulfilling orders from the Middle East – especially from Iran, Jordan and Libya. Popular culture at the time featured songs by Bob Dylan and his 'Masters of War' alongside Donovan's 'Universal Soldier', and they were major influences on me. There was something wrong here.

The upshot of this was that I decided that I could not spend my life in the arms business. There were few opportunities in N Ireland at that time and I generally applied for jobs in England. I also applied for Voluntary Service Overseas. I can remember at the interview being asked about something to do with religion and I said that I was an atheist. It was probably the first time I had said it out loud.

Two weeks later they offered me a two-year posting as a senior lecturer at the Hardy Senior Technical Institute (HSTI) in Eastern Ceylon (now Sri Lanka). It was with some trepidation that I wrote back accepting. Serendipity – out of the frying pan into the fire.

Apart from the fact that it produced tea, I knew nothing of Ceylon and I certainly hadn't expected to be going from a country with one religio-political problem into another that was almost identical. To a first approximation, the situation in Ceylon paralleled that in N Ireland in that the ruling majority party in government was closely aligned with one religious and cultural-linguistic group. Various laws, including the "Sinhala language only" law, had had the effect of favouring Buddhists who generally spoke Sinhala and disadvantaging the Hindus, Moslems and Christians who mainly spoke Tamil (or English). At the same time the government was experiencing a separate problem from a "Maoist anti-Imperialist" insurgency. This movement, the Janata Vimukhti Peramuna (JVP) People's Liberation Front, was mainly led by students and thought to be backed by North Korea and China. This anti-imperialist philosophy was also supported by some more Buddhist monks who thought that the government was not "Ceylonist" enough.

Thousands died, mainly youths, and many more had been tortured and imprisoned. Bizarrely the Chinese and N Korean governments (along with many others, including the UK) had been pro-active in providing military support to the government to quash the movement.

My travel date was delayed for several months because of this uprising but in October 1971 I flew to Colombo and then on to the Eastern side of the island in an old, rattly, DC3 Dakota.

The eastern side of Sri Lanka is very different from the warm, humid, lush and densely populated Western side of the island. Although hotter it is also less humid and mainly scrub jungle. For over a thousand years a series of enormous earthwork "tanks", reservoirs which stored water collected during the monsoons, had provided irrigation for subsistence farmers in the area. Many of these tanks and their waterways had fallen into disuse – epidemics of cholera and malaria as well as drought often decimating the population over the centuries, but in the 1950s, as part of a "Let the deserts bloom" programme, a large dam had been constructed. This dam now provided a year round supply of water for cultivation of crops including the rice staple. It also provided hydroelectric power sufficient for a number of industries including a sugar processing plant and a paper mill.

Hardy Senior Technical Institute (HSTI) had been set up by Professor Evans Hardy in the 1950s as part of this grand plan and was designed to provide the managers, agriculturalists and engineers who would create and maintain the infrastructure. In its hey-day it had been a model technical institute attracting students from all over Asia but after its driving force and provider of foreign funding Professor Evans suddenly died it had declined.

To some extent this decline was a consequence of the initial spectacular success of the programme. With the availability of newly irrigated and now very productive land, Sinhala-speaking Buddhists had moved into what had previously been a mainly Tamil area. As a consequence, there was some ethnic tension between the groups and technical specialists were very reluctant to relocate there. Indeed that was one reason why I was there.

Not everyone was Buddhist or Tamil. A thin strip of the coastal area was substantially Muslim, descendants of Arab traders, and there were some Malayans who had developed a separate Creole language. There were also a small number of Roman Catholics and "Christians" (in Ceylon the term "Christian" was reserved for protestants). Many of these were descendent of Dutch traders, the "Burghers", often identifiable by their pale skin. Some Veddas were even reputed still to be living in the jungle, the oldest indigenous forest-dwelling inhabitants, who still hunted with bows and arrows and were animists.

Our closest English neighbour was a Methodist missionary who lived about thirty miles away on the coast in Kalmunai. Unlike the missionaries, whom I remember coming to our church when I was young, and who always seemed to combine extreme piety with dourness, Barbara Atkins was a lovely bubbly lady who was soon to retire and go back to the UK. She was dreading it. She had left England in her twenties and over forty years had established and run an orphanage. As she said, in those days when you came here it was for life, and then she would giggle. She giggled a lot! She was also extremely good at Scrabble.

I don't know what became of her or her life's work. Much of the civil war that started a few years later and affected Sri Lanka over the next 40 years or so raged along that coastline. Then on 26th December 2004 the Asian tsunami struck the east coast of Sri Lanka. Kalmunai, the most easterly point and most vulnerable, was decimated.

Nature is pretty indifferent to culture, language and belief.

Humanism and SIFRE – I'd been an atheist since my late teens but that was it. Generally atheists don't get together as group to share their disbelief, I suppose in the same way as people who don't collect stamps don't feel a need to share their disinterest in philately.

Over the years there had been some niggles. My children had not been able to go to the nearest primary school (C of E) as, unlike others, we had been honest in filling in the application form. As my sons grew up I had become very active in supporting the local cub and scout group. I had been a Queen's scout in my youth. However, I was not allowed to be a leader because atheists were prohibited from being anything other than helpers.

It was only comparatively recently that I started to think that things could and should be different. As with many people, the trigger was a Humanist funeral. My parents had both died within a year or so of each other and we had gone through the motions of having typical and traditional Northern Irish (protestant) funerals. What surprised me was that even though the minister knew both my parents, it didn't really show. I had written the eulogies, bits of which he embellished to emphasise their Christian credentials. I am sure he was well meaning but the services were so peppered with religious overtones that they were not really about them. After one of them, one of my cousins commented, "Too many commercials." It might not have seemed a particularly appropriate remark in the circumstances but I thought it summed up my feelings exactly.

Several years later I attended a Humanist funeral. This time it was for one of my mother's cousins who lived in Lincolnshire. The Celebrant began with "Tom said that he wanted no bullshit at his funeral..." That not only summed up Tom's self-deprecating nature but almost brought the house down and set the tone for the whole event. I have never been to a funeral that felt so right. I Googled "Humanism" when I returned home and realized that my views aligned pretty well with everything I found there.

I had been a Humanist for years but not realised it.

I joined the British Humanist Association (BHA) and the local group, Suffolk Humanists and Secularists (SHANDS). Through SHANDS, I became involved with both the local Standing Advisory Committee for Religious Education (SACRE) and SIFRE. While I do not consider

Humanism to be a religion, both of these bodies accept that many people are non-religious and that theirs is an important world-view and are as valid as those of any religious persuasion.

I doubt if anybody is ever converted to Humanism, or atheism for that matter. It is something you work out for yourself using all the information and evidence that is available. For me, the essence of Humanism – trust in the scientific method, evidence, and reason and to place human welfare and happiness at the centre of ethical decision-making – is far more important than the need to believe in any form of god or gods, or to have a religious belief. For me that is more than enough to bring happiness and meaning to life.

# Derek Mason: It all remains a mystery

Six years old, in church, surrounded by adults who are all facing in one direction, singing hymns, praying, I tried to see who was the target of all this effort, but there was no one there! I did not understand, and seventy-two years later, I still don't. What is this belief that defies logic and reasoning?

Later in life, I attended school assemblies because it was compulsory but didn't join in with any religious aspects. I hoped someone would question my rebelliousness, but nobody commented.

I avoid the labels that seem necessary to define a person, such as atheist and agnostic, because they are interpreted as opposed to religion. I am not opposed; I just do not understand it. In the same way, I do not understand quantum physics, but I'm not opposed to it.

I have never knowingly harmed anyone, physically or mentally, which cannot be said of many people of faith. Thousands, perhaps millions, have been killed in the name of religion. There has never been an atheist war.

On the rare occasions that I've discussed religion with a person of faith, I've asked if God made everything. The answer was always "Yes". I then asked why he made, for example, cancer. End of conversation. It all remains a mystery.

*Derek died in July 2013.*
*His thoughts, above, were read at his Humanist funeral.*

# Elizabeth Sugarman: Being Jewish in Suffolk

As a child and young adult I moved around the country and lived in many areas with and without thriving Jewish communities. My move to Suffolk was work related and meant relocating from Sussex very near to an active Jewish community in Brighton, where at that time there were four synagogues, to Suffolk, a place with no synagogue. I knew that if I accepted a job I would have to travel to find a synagogue and although I was aware of one in Colchester I was unable to locate it and so journeyed to Norwich as often as possible. Eventually I found the Colchester synagogue and was made very welcome there, so much so that for many years I made a round trip of approximately one hundred miles to join the Shabbat evening service on a Friday evening and went most weeks. There were also festivals and other events that took me there. We now have a small community that meets in Ipswich about once a month on a Friday and for some festivals. I continue with my membership at Colchester.

So in some ways the move to Suffolk has helped to strengthen my belief in Judaism, as I have had to make more of an effort to maintain any relationship with a community. When the community is on one's doorstep so to speak it is relatively easy to practise the faith. Kosher provisions are an issue as they are not readily available in Suffolk. The fact that I have to drive to a synagogue and that kosher food is not to be found in Suffolk rules me out as an Orthodox Jew. Judaism, as with many faiths, has a spectrum of observance from Ultra-Orthodox through Orthodox and Reform to Liberal. Over the years I have thought of myself as Jewish without any of the labels that are usually associated with being a member of a particular community. Therefore I am comfortable and happy in any Jewish community.

Once I retired from full-time employment I became more actively involved with interfaith work through my association with The Suffolk

Inter-Faith Resource (SIFRE), going into schools to contribute to religious education by giving talks on Judaism to children from reception class through to year 12, and participating in whole school assemblies. My involvement with SIFRE has also enabled me to talk about Judaism within further and higher education, and with diversity training for the police, fire service and local government services. One of the areas that I have particularly enjoyed has been speaking to people of other faiths about Judaism and learning from them about their faith. In many ways knowing more about other faiths and beliefs has confirmed my belief in Judaism. This has been particularly so when I have visited churches of different denominations and discussed with their members the similarities and differences between Judaism and Christianity.

My involvement in inter-faith activities has shown me just how many similarities there are among the many faiths that exist. There are differences but I think that the majority of people, regardless of their faith or beliefs, wish for a better life for all and for the ultimate gift of universal peace.

Somehow, in 2004, I became a member of the Suffolk Standing Advisory Council on Religious Education (SACRE). Each SACRE has representation from faiths other than Christianity and I represent the local Jewish community on the council. SACREs provide support for teachers in their delivery of the RE curriculum and in the provision of collective worship. Since October 2010 I have chaired SACRE. I am one of only a handful of non-Christian chairmen of SACREs in England and feel very fortunate to live in a place so welcoming of people of different beliefs and cultures.

In addition to SACRE I am part of the multi-faith chaplaincy teams at Ipswich Hospital and Suffolk New College and University Campus Suffolk. In both of these roles I am there to offer support to people of all faiths and none. The Jewish community in Suffolk is quite small and therefore I rarely have to respond to the needs of my own faith community. Occasionally I have also spoken to Women's Institute groups and the Mothers' Union, thereby increasing my involvement in the wider community. All these activities have helped to strengthen my own beliefs.

# Frank Bright:

# Growing up under German Occupation

I was introduced as Frank Bright. I wasn't always Frank Bright. That is my anglicised name. People found my original name difficult to pronounce, I had to spell it all the time, I felt that I ought to make life easier for my fellow men and women, as well as for myself, and so I changed it by deed poll in 1952.

My name at birth was Franz Brichta, my place of birth was Berlin and my date of birth was October 1928, which makes me nearly 85 years of age. Here is my birth certificate. It is in Gothic script. The Germans, even in their pre-Nazi era, wanted to be different, thought of themselves as better than anybody else, looked down on everybody else and one way of doing that was to have what we now call a "font" of their own, even if it is far more ornate and not as easy to read as the plain Roman script used by everybody else.

What you ought to bear in mind is that, with such a birth certificate, issued to a Jewish baby around that time, came a death sentence, a death sentence carried out without compunction, or the slightest hesitation, on those, to the German mind, of an inferior race. I use the word "race" on purpose because the Germans did not recognise "faith" as defining whether a man, woman or child was Jewish or German, or rather "Aryan". In that respect, I am an exception, I am one of the very few who escaped the death sentence, and it was not for want of trying by the Germans. I am an exception which proves the rule. The rule was that a Jewish child did not survive. Of the 6 million Jews murdered by the Germans, 1½ million were children.

"Aryan", or "Arier" in German, was the important term the Germans used to define their own race as distinct from other, and to their mind inferior, races. Jews, by their definition were not, and could not be Germans, even though German Jews had fought in the German army, air force and navy during the First World War and had done so for what they believed was their fatherland and for their emperor.

My grandfather, on my mother's side, had been a Prussian volunteer during the Franco-Prussian war of 1870-1871. He did so because he considered himself to be, and his fellow Prussians agreed with it at the time, first and foremost a Prussian, one of the Jewish religion. His son, my uncle Fritz, served in the German navy throughout the First World War and was decorated with an Iron Cross. In gratitude for services rendered he was sent to Auschwitz and death on 3rd March 1943 after he and his wife, my aunt, had to carry out forced labour for at least three years, in the Berlin branches of armament factories. They were made to live in a sparsely furnished room, were not permitted into air-raid shelters during the many air-raids, had to walk to work, had fewer rations than everybody else, could not buy shoes or protective clothing because Jews did not receive clothing coupons, could only do their shopping between 4 and 5 in the afternoon. On 21st January 1939 they had to hand in all of their jewellery, items made of gold, silver, platinum, and pearls. In his previous life he had worked his way up and had been a director of the Dresdner Bank.

All this sincere attempt by Jews to assimilate, to win Nobel prizes for Germany, to win medals at the Olympic Games for Germany, to fight and to die for Germany, all this was swept aside, not only by the

Nazi party, but also by the many Germans who had voted the Nazi party into power, thus providing it with the largest number of seats in the German parliament.

Until that moment everything the Nazi party had achieved had been achieved legitimately by democratic means. Nobody had forced the German people to vote for the Nazi party; they had done so quite voluntarily, of their own free will, because the Nazi programme had appealed to them.

# German federal election, November 1932
From Wikipedia, the free encyclopedia

The **German parliamentary election of 6 November 1932** saw a slight drop for the Nazi Party and increases for the KPD and DNVP. Although the Nazis remained the largest party they were still outnumbered by the Social Democrats and Communists.

This election was the last relatively free and fair all-German election until the reunification of Germany and the election of December 1990.

**Germany**

This article is part of the series:
**Politics and government of Germany**

| Party | Vote percentage (change) | | Seats (change) | |
|---|---|---|---|---|
| National Socialist German Workers Party (NSDAP) | 33.1% | -4.2% | 196 | -34 |
| Social Democratic Party of Germany (SPD) | 20.4% | -1.2% | 121 | -12 |
| Communist Party of Germany (KPD) | 16.9% | +2.6% | 100 | +11 |
| Centre Party (Z) | 11.9% | -0.5% | 70 | -5 |
| German National People's Party (DNVP) | 8.5% | +2.6% | 52 | +15 |
| Bavarian People's Party (BVP) | 3.1% | -0.1% | 20 | -2 |
| German People's Party (DVP) | 1.9% | -0.1% | 11 | +4 |
| Christian Social People's Service | 1.1% | +0.1% | 5 | +2 |
| German Farmers' Party (DBP) | 0.4% | +/-0 | 3 | +1 |
| German Democratic Party (DDP) | 1.0% | +/-0 | 2 | -2 |
| Agricultural League | 0.3% | +/-0 | 2 | +/-0 |
| Reich Party of the German Middle Class (WP) | 0.3% | -0.1% | 1 | -1 |
| German-Hanoverian Party (DHP) | 0.2% | +0.1% | 1 | +1 |
| Other | 0.9% | +0.3% | 0 | -2 |
| **Totals** | **100.0%** | | **584** | **-24** |

**Constitution**

- Constitution
- Human rights

**Legislature**

- Federal Convention (Bundesversammlung)
- Federal Council (Bundesrat)
- Federal Diet (Bundestag)

**Judiciary**

- Constitutional Court
- Administrative Court
- Court of Justice (ordinary jurisdiction)
- Finance Court
- Labor Court
- Social court

**Executive**

- President
  - Christian Wulff
- Chancellor
  - Angela Merkel

What was the Nazi programme which won them the election of the 6th of November 1932? It was first and foremost rearmament on a vast scale, a large standing army, a most modern air force, the construction of a fleet of the most modern battleships, U-Boats, supply ships, motor-torpedo boats, tanks of all types and guns of every type of which the 88mm gun has never been surpassed both as an artillery piece and as an anti-aircraft gun. They wanted another war. They had done everything to prepare for and to win the First World War and had lost. They needed a scapegoat for that loss.

Naturally, they should not have started World War One which resulted in their invasion of Belgium and of Northern France, particularly of Flanders, which was completely demolished, burnt and churned up. They didn't want to see it that way or that their war had not taken place on German soil. They could have blamed their field marshals and generals for their incompetence. They didn't want to see it that way either.

As had been the case for over a thousand years, the Jews were turned into scapegoats and that fell on very receptive ears.

Thus the Nazi programme consisted, apart from their vast rearmament works, of a virulent anti-Semitism. Jews were blamed for every one of their misfortunes, real or imagined, under the sun. The purpose of this virulent and criminal anti-Semitism was two-fold; firstly to remove Jews from every post. Right from the beginning, within three months after they had usurped absolute power, the universities, primary and secondary schools, the stage, orchestras, the judiciary, the civil service, were purged of Jews who were dismissed without a pension, and authors, doctors, veterinary surgeons, medical doctors, lawyers, dentists, pharmacists, art dealers, etc., were prohibited from carrying on their profession. That resulted, as intended, of jobs for the boys and penury for Jews. Shops, workshops, factories, laboratories, farm, woodlands, any property, were "Aryanised". That meant that the owners were simply turfed out. That too resulted in jobs for the boys. The aim was to remove Jews from all of civic life and to turn them into outcasts, only fit for forced labour in the many armament factories with names like Siemens, Benz, BMW, AEG, Volkswagen, etc. The propaganda theme was that Jews were exploiting Germans. The fact was that Germans exploited Jews. The other purpose was to rob Jews of every item of their possessions.

The Nuremberg Laws of 1935 forbade the marriage between Jews and Germans and also defined the status of children of a "mixed" marriage, classifying them into "Mischlinge", or of "mixed" race, of the first and second degree. I was only a common or garden Jewish child but for those from a so-called mixed marriage the degree of Aryan blood mattered.

For instance, Fritz Behrendt and his elder brother Hans had only one Jewish grandmother. They were thus of the second degree. Both had to serve in the German air force but were not sent to the front as their 16% impurity of blood precluded them from dying a hero's death for the Führer. Thus they survived thanks to their Jewish grandmother.

It took next to no time to construct concentration camps. The first one, Dachau, near Munich, was opened on the 9th of March 1933. Starting from 30th January 1933, the day Hitler became Chancellor and promptly took on dictatorial powers by declaring a state of emergency, it had taken 5 weeks for its torture chambers to receive their first victims. They dispensed with planning permission and public consultation. Both were superfluous anyway, the German people, or Volk, agreed with its construction, and with all subsequent ones anyway, and plenty of sadistic operators were found to flog, beat, starve, torture, hang and shoot its innocent prisoners without having to advertise and interview for such jobs.

They also made sure that the terror they inflicted became well known very quickly and the letters KZ (Ka-Tset) and what they represented, became a threat overnight. It even frightened a 5-year old, like me. Just like the word "hell" in medieval times, it was not precisely defined but certainly sounded evil and was to be feared. In Dante's Inferno the inscription above the entrance to hell, "Abandon hope, you who enter here", would have been far more appropriate for the entrance to any of the many German concentration camps than the cynical "Work sets you free".

I started primary school in April 1935, at the age of 6½. It was a Jewish school, newly established to absorb those Jewish children whose stay at German schools had been made impossible by the brutality of their Aryan German classmates and of their teachers. Referring again to Fritz Behrendt and his brother, both of whom were older than me and who had transferred from just such a school to my school, on the day after Hitler had been made chancellor their teacher appeared in the SA's brown shirt uniform and told the class about the "new era" which was to unfold, and fellow pupils too appeared in the uniform of the Hitlerjugend, bought by their parents well in advance of the day they had been looking forward to. National Socialism, the proper name for Nazism, its abbreviated form, was not forced on Germans, they took to it, and to the criminal outlook it stood for, like ducks take to water.

I now know that my first-year teacher committed suicide in 1942, preferring an overdose of sleeping tablets to being sent East and murdered there. My second and third year teacher had to carry out forced labour for a removal firm after the school was closed in June of 1942; after that he was sent to Auschwitz and death in January of 1943.

To emigrate, to get out, to flee, to save your family and yourself from a constantly worsening situation, was the answer which dawned on most Jews once they had realised that their honestly and sincerely held belief that they were Germans had proved to have been an illusion. But it was only a theoretical answer. The real and actual problems facing would-be emigrants were manifold and often impossible to overcome, apart from family ties and the human desire and duty to look after elderly parents.

1. The Germans demanded an exit tax which you had to pay before you were issued with a passport – a passport which had a large "J" printed inside it, something the Swiss had insisted on. You had to pay that tax, or Reichsfluchtsteuer, the tax on fleeing Germany, before they issued an exit permit. That tax left you poor.

2. You needed a visa from a foreign government. Foreign governments didn't want poor immigrants, although being a Jew was the greatest obstacle.

3. In fact foreign governments didn't want any Jews. Full stop. Our plight was well known. Until the outbreak of the war reporters were free to come and go and report to their newspapers what they saw. It made no difference.

Canada said that one Jewish immigrant was one too many.

Australia had a "whites only" policy and, following the German example, Jews were not recognised as being white. That continued until well after the war.

South Africa had a racist policy of her own and had a Boer, i.e. a pro-German government. After all the Germans had helped the Boers to fight the British during the Boer War (1899-1902).

The South American republics demanded a baptism certificate, something Jews could obviously not provide. On the other hand members of the SS did provide such certificates and entered South America in droves, including Eichmann.

The United States were particularly obstructive. They had a system of annual quotas, meant to keep Jews out, which it did. They were not going to budge. A typical example were the Blochs. They lived on the ground floor of our block of flats in Prague and had registered for immigration at the US Consulate in Prague after the German occupation of March 1939. The parents were murdered in Auschwitz in 1943. Only their son Gottfried survived and that only because he was a young medical doctor although he had been prevented from taking his finals by the German students of the German Charles University in Prague, which Gottfried had attended. The Nazis were in control even before the invasion. He went through the ghetto, Auschwitz and Buchenwald. He wrote a book on his experiences called 'Unfree Associations, a Psychoanalyst Recollects the Holocaust'. I can recommend it.

It took 17 years before his turn for a US entry visa came up. By that time he had got married, had a daughter, had lived in Israel since 1949 and was a psychologist attached to the Israeli Defence Force. Anybody applying in 1939 needed it then and there. There would not be any other applications for the next six years anyway, although that was unforeseeable. To make you wait longer, knowing full well what the situation was, meant that you were not wanted.

There is an inscription at the base of the Statue of Liberty in New York Harbour. It is by Emma Lazarus, a Jewish American poetess. It reads, "Give me your tired, your poor, your huddled masses yearning to breathe free." But that applied only to the huddled masses who were not Jewish.

Then there was Palestine, the obvious choice for historical and religious reasons, for Jews, particularly for young Jews, to make the desert bloom again after centuries of Arab and Turkish neglect, and to establish a state there to avoid having to ask others for protection in the case of persecution and receiving a cold shoulder.

The old story of Israel is a sad one. Israel took on the might of the Roman Empire and, not surprisingly, lost. But it is also difficult to argue that it could have done anything else. It resulted in the destruction of the second Temple, the carting away of the Temple treasures, as can be seen to this day in stone on the Arch of Titus in Rome. There was the dispersion of its inhabitants although many stayed on. The early Christian writers, certainly the gospel writers who were Jews, wrote around 100 AD.

Then came the Arab Muslim conquerors; then, for a short time, the Crusaders around 1100 AD. The Crusaders murdered Jews. The Crusaders were defeated by Saladin and 600 of the knights who had surrendered were beheaded. Saladin decreed that each of his Muslim clerics had to behead at least one Christian Crusader. That explains the way a British soldier was murdered recently in London.

Then came the Turks who let the country go to waste until their Ottoman Empire fell apart in 1917.

General Allenby took Palestine from the Turks and occupied Palestine, all of it, both sides of the River Jordan. The then British Prime Minister, Lord Balfour, declared that all of that area would once more become a Jewish homeland.

Although the League of Nations and other international conferences confirmed that, Britain went back on her word and created, quite unilaterally, the Kingdom of Jordan and prohibited the settling of Jews on that side of the Jordan, restricting them to the narrow strip between the Jordan and the Mediterranean Sea.

Around 1935 the Mufti of Jerusalem, a great friend of Herr Hitler, started the Arab Revolt. Please note that it was called the Arab Revolt, not the Palestinian Revolt. Everybody who lived there at the time, Jew, Christian and Arab, was "a Palestinian". The revolt, quite violent, was against Jewish immigration. Arab violence, which meant and means murder of farmers tilling their fields as well as shooting dead British administration officers, is nothing new. In 1929 they slaughtered Jews in Hebron and, rather than protect the remainder, the British ordered them to leave. A campaign of terrorism also started in 1929 with the call to the Arab masses of "Izbah Al-Yahud!" – "Slaughter the Jews!" Nothing has changed.

The response to the Arab Revolt was the usual Commission of Enquiry and its Report, a White Paper. The easy way out, the way usually taken, was to cave in to Arab demands by restricting Jewish immigration to a trickle, or to put it another way, shut the door in our faces at the hour of our greatest need.

It is also perfectly true to say that those prevented from entering Palestine went up through the chimneys of Auschwitz. The Arabs may not have done so themselves but they did so vicariously, they let the Germans do it. But for the Arab Revolt at least a hundred thousand would have found a safe haven there. Anybody trying to enter Palestine before, during and after the war was apprehended and imprisoned on the charge of being an "illegal immigrant" and sent to an old prison on the island of Mauritius where many died. Those who survived this open-ended sentence were not released at the end of the war either. Only on the establishment of the State of Israel three years later was that done. Their crime? To have tried to escape from the Nazis. That was an offence so horrid that it could only be countered with an administrative order, not with a proper trial, a judge and a jury or what is called "due process", available to any petty thief but not to Jews.

The book, the film and the real story of the immigrant ship, an old rusty bucket only fit for the scrap yard, the Exodus was one of many. It was intercepted on the high seas by the Royal Navy which returned its passengers, all survivors of the Holocaust, to camps in Germany and on the island of Cyprus, where they were put once again behind barbed wire. It is also true that, while Bomber Command put their lives on the line every day and night and received no recognition at all until last year, the crew of RN ships which hunted down and imprisoned defenceless Jews received a medal for their participation in the "Palestine Patrol". With friends like that, who needed enemies?

It is not surprising that as a young person I felt "not wanted", an "outsider" and "not belonging" to a people who had a home or a state or a country of their own.

So what do I remember of Berlin between, say 1934, when I was 6 years old, and 1938, when we left Prague and I was 9 years old.

First of all there were those cartoons in display cases at street corners showing terribly ugly Jews doing apparently terrible things to very innocent looking German boys and girls. In these cartoons, the Jews sported either a Soviet Russian army cap or a top hat covered with the Stars and Stripes, thus accusing Jews of being Bolsheviks (an earlier name for Communists) or being Plutocrats (another name for Capitalists). I found both versions confusing and threatening. Even I knew that German youth in their Hitlerjugend uniforms were anything but innocent because they sang "Wenn's Judenblut vom Messer spritzt dann gehts nochmal so gut", which roughly translates as "When Jewish blood squirts from the knife things can only improve".

I also knew that Communism and Capitalism are mutually exclusive. If we are being accused of being both at the same time then the cartoonist got it all wrong. Also, and adding to confusion, none of my Jewish relatives, friends, acquaintances, schoolmates, present or past as seen on family photos, were ugly, some were positively good looking. Looking back at one of the few photos I have of myself of which my first day at school is an example, did I look anything like the way the German cartoonist portrayed me and every other Jew? If he was wrong in that then he was wrong in everything else. Yet that was standard German propaganda fare and they believed it and Dr Göbbels, their Propaganda, or improper-ganda Minister, was cheered to the rafters every time he spewed this bilge.

I also remember that everybody was in uniform, the SA in brown, the brown shirts, the SS in black, the army in field grey with their jackboots with which they intended to trample all over Europe, something they soon did, the Hitler Youth in brown. Uniforms meant war. By 1933 they wanted war. The last one had come to an end only 15 years earlier. What sort of mentality was that?

Then there were war-like toys for tiny tots. German children didn't play with rubber ducks in the bath, they played with toy submarines.

Wound up they would dive and surface at the far end of the bath. I had one. I also had a toy bomber which, when wound up, would fly round and round, suspended from a string fixed to the ceiling, and drop four bombs loaded with percussion caps one after another. A portent of things to come, though they didn't realise that it would happen to them as well.

I remember an air-raid exercise using a small phosphor incendiary bomb, at a time when the rest of Europe wanted peace.

I was the product of my environment. From the very beginning to the end of the war, when I was 16½, I experienced nothing but threats, violence and was looked upon as sub-human. I experienced discrimination, hunger and deprivation. I was done out of an education, robbed of everything, and saw the perpetrators go free and die in their beds – something they had denied to us.

I have to go quickly over my early days in Prague and the Munich Agreement which sealed our fate and that of Europe and Russia. It most certainly did not provide the "peace in our time" and "peace with honour" as pronounced by Prime Minister Neville Chamberlain waving a piece of paper while alighting from a plane after talks with Herr Hitler who had assured that gullible man that "he had no further territorial demands". The handing over of the Sudeten part of the Czechoslovak Republic, or the giving away of land which wasn't his to give away, had serious consequences, costing the lives of millions of people, quite apart from the 6 million Jews, and it also enabled the Soviet Empire to expand into Europe and to rule behind the Iron Curtain for over 40 years.

Prague in 1938 was full of poor refugees. There were Jews from Germany, from Austria which had been incorporated into the Reich in March of 1938 to the jubilant acclamation of its non-Jewish population, and from the Sudeten, which had likewise been incorporated into the German Reich in October of 1938 by an act of treason. These refugees had nowhere else to go because, as already mentioned and as embedded in my psyche, nobody wanted them.

They were allowed to enter but that was all the Czechs could, or would, do. They had troubles of their own. All of us were trapped.

A quick look at the map of the lay of the land after Munich shows the trap. Bohemia and Moravia was surrounded by an aggressive Germany on all sides. To seal its fate completely, Slovakia declared independence under a Catholic parish priest, who was also the leader of a fascist party, father Tišo. He called on Herr Hitler for assistance, which the latter naturally and gladly provided; it had been his idea in the first place. It was like playing drafts. One piece after another disappeared from the map, sometimes two or three were taken at the same time.

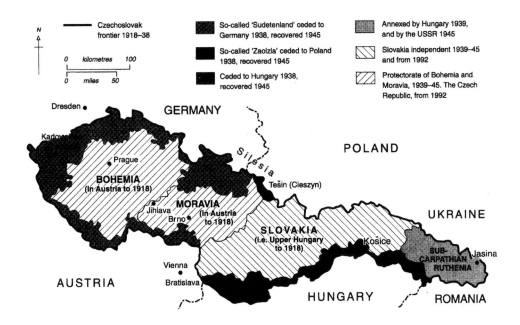

We rented a small one-bedroom flat in a newly finished 6-storey block, I started to learn Czech and also started to attend a Jewish school again and we lived, and suffered, under the ever-increasing list of restrictions. Anything from fewer rations, no clothing coupons, a short shopping hour in the afternoon, a curfew at 8pm, having to wear a yellow star, being prohibited from using public transport, from using telephones, having to hand in radios, bicycles, sewing machines, typewriters, musical instruments, also gramophones and records, woollens, cameras, binoculars, not being allocated shaving soap, nor any type of fruit and fish or onions, even dried ones, prohibited from visiting a barber and barbers being prohibited from visiting Jews. We were not permitted to read Czech newspapers and to be found in possession of a German paper was a criminal offence. There were streets which were closed to us, as were swimming pools, hospitals and attendance at public performances. Jewish doctors, lawyers, patent agents, veterinary surgeons, dentists and dental technicians, teachers, professors, chemists, etc. were permitted to cater to Jewish clients only and only a very small number were allowed to practice at all. The contents of doctors' and dentists' surgeries were seized. Bank accounts were frozen; shares were seized, as were life policies and savings accounts.

We had to hand in all items made of precious metal including gold, platinum and silver as well as diamonds and pearls, e.g. pocket watches with fob and chain, as men used to wear, necklaces, rings, tie pins, silver cigarette cases, (people, at least men, used to smoke), ear rings, bracelets, the lot.

Records were kept and are available on the internet – see the following two pages. I worked out that, using January 2012 prices, the value of that robbery from that small area alone was worth over £78 million. To that one has to add the loot from German, Austrian, Polish, Russian, French, Dutch, Belgian and other Jews and the value of the loot is enormous. No offer of restitution or compensation was ever made to even the few survivors.

Here I must add that not only were we constantly hungry, the bread ration was far too small, but the total absence of vegetables, fruit and fish meant that we had no access to vitamins and minerals and therefore the body's resistance to bacterial infection was reduced and we were very prone to boils. Small cuts which one does not even notice to-day turned septic.

List of Property seized by Germany from Jews in the territory of Bohemia and Moravia occupied between 15.03.1939 and 08.05.1945, known as the "Protektorat".

Translation of parts (addresses of Treuhand stores omitted) of pages 295, 326, 327, etc. of the research book by "Historia Nova" :

Jews in the German Protectorate of Bohemia and Moravia, Report of the Jewish Community for the year 1942 – Documents, published in Prague in 1997.

Summary of confiscated goods deposited in the various Treuhand stores as of December 1942. Figures in brackets are the final number of the particular item estimated to be seized after the end of 1942 when all Jewish families would have been deported and their dwellings completely emptied.

| Type | Quantities | |
| --- | --- | --- |
| Complete surgeries of Jewish doctors | 828 | |
| Medical instruments and medicines | 51,734 | (144,734) |
| Pictures, ordinary | 34,652 | (53,680) |
| Books | 547,458 | (1,532,460) |
| Electrical Appliances | 22,012 | (61,612) |
| Eating utensils, whole matching sets | 2,212 | (6,193) |
| Bicycles | 3,503 | |
| Photographic instruments | 7,484 | (7,551) |
| Glass and porcelain | 364,993 | (1,021,990) |
| House and kitchen utensils | 1,045,088 | (2,926,088) |
| Suitcases, (usually leather) | 3,151 | (8,820) |
| Refrigerators, powered | 116 | 324 |
| Works of art | 10,455 | (29,258) |
| Groceries and cleaning material | 41,113 | (115,113) |

| Type | | |
|---|---:|---:|
| Tins and preserving jars | 6,317 | (17,687) |
| Do. in Kg. | 8,429 | (18,608) |
| Empty boxes | 6,325 | |
| Leather goods | 17,050 | (47,740) |
| Linoleum | 1,334 | (3,735) |
| Measuring and technical instruments | 3,924 | (10,987) |
| Musical instruments, Not portable, e.g. pianos | 439 | (1,220) |
| Musical instruments, portable, i.e. string wind, brass, gramophones, records | 20,870 | (56,436) |
| Sewing machines | 1,159 | (3,239) |
| Optical instruments | 15,560 | (43,568) |
| Furs, and items made of fur | 34,543 | |
| Children's toys | 3,260 | (9,128) |
| Fabrics and feather quilts | 1,025,496 | (2,871,496) |
| Ditto scraps, tons | 4.8 | |
| Ditto, lengths miles | 2.62 | |
| Typewriters | 2,036 | |
| Shoes, in pairs and single | 38,788 | |
| Carpets | 18,958 | (52,985) |
| Clocks | 4,989 | (13,970) |

Then the dreaded transports started. First to the ghetto of Lodž in Poland, where out of 5,000 people only 276 lived to see liberation. After those first five transports everybody was sent first to the ghetto of Theresienstadt, or Terezín in Czech, which was really a transit camp with constant coming and going.

I shall give you a few statistics which you should not find boring because every one of them was a human being worthy of life and whose life was brutally extinguished by Germans after they had been exploited and all of their property had been taken.

### The population of the Ghetto of Theresienstadt/Terezín from 24 November 1941 to 20 April 1945

|  | Protektorat | Germany | Austria | Holland | Other | Total |
|---|---|---|---|---|---|---|
| Inmates of The ghetto | 73 468 | 42 921 | 15 244 | 4 897 | 2987 | 139 517 |
| Born in the Ghetto | 167 | 35 | 3 | - | - | 205 |
| Died in the Ghetto | 6 152 | 20 848 | 6 228 | 168 | 124 | 33 521 |
| Deported to the East | 60 382 | 16 098 | 7 572 | 3 010 | 1 | 87 063 |
| Evacuated by Swiss or Swedes | 101 | 523 | 153 | 433 | 413 | 1 623 |
| Situation On 20.04.1945 | 7 000 | 5 487 | 1 294 | 1 285 | 2 449 | 17 515 |

Looking only at the German-occupied so-called Protectorate of Bohemia and Moravia, 114 transports left the area between 16th October 1941 and the 13th July 1943, a period of 21 months or one transport every 5 to 6 days. On board were 75,630 Jewish men women and children of whom 69,772 were murdered and 6,362 survived until liberation. The average death rate was 91.6% or for every 1,000 persons deported 916 were murdered. And that from a small area which you have a job trying to find on a map.

Those who arrived in the transit ghetto of Theresienstadt faced the real prospect of further transportation to the unknown East from which no traveller had ever returned. Of the 139, 517 Jews who arrived in the ghetto from the Protectorate, from Germany, from Austria, Holland and Denmark 87, 063 were deported to the East, first to extermination camps, later to Auschwitz where some were selected for slave labour.

There were 63 transports from the ghetto to the East between 9th January 1942 and 28th October 1944, or within 2 years and 9 months. Of the over 87,000 men women and children sent East from the ghetto 3,097 survived, an average death rate of 96½%, or a survival rate of 3½%. That is an average and should be put into the context of extermination. Thus: Of 10 transports carrying 18,004 people to Treblinka during September and October 1942 not a single person survived, and of 3 transports carrying 3,000 people to Trostinec during August and September 1942 only one person survived.

Some, mostly who were not there, call the ghetto of Thersienstadt a concentration camp and also that it was all singing and dancing, just because it suited the Germans to hand out a few musical instruments which they had already looted from Jewish homes. That is nonsense. It was, as I have shown, first and foremost a transit camp where many people, most of the elderly, died. They were starved to death and, if they came

*Plundered instruments in Prague.*

from Germany, arrived in an already weak state. Thus of the 139, 517 who arrived in the ghetto 33,521 died in the ghetto, that is 24% or a quarter. That is an average. If we look at it more closely then, of the 42,921 Jews from Germany, no fewer than 20,848 or 48.6% died in the ghetto, and that is nearly half.

In the ghetto I shared a small room with 6 other boys of my age and I worked in a workshop repairing locks and making keys and hinges. My parents were separated. My mother had to share a large room in one of the old brick barrack buildings dating from the 1790s with something like a hundred women, all coughing, sneezing, talking in their sleep and snoring, with those near the window wanting it shut and those away from the window wanting it open. There were double bunks very close together without any space for one's few belongings. For years in Prague she had been on her own all day, looking forward to our return from work and school. To her, being suddenly among so many strangers must have been particularly painful. My father

shared a smaller, but still claustrophobic, room with other men. At least one still had one's own clothes, even if few of them, as the duffle bag one was allowed to bring into the ghetto was small and most of that space was taken up with the blankets one was recommended to pack.

For me it was unpleasant being torn from the familiar four walls which gave one privacy and being turfed into the turmoil and conditions of the ghetto, being separated from one's parents, not being able to help them and seeing them suffer, mainly from hunger. Everything though is relative. In spite of the privations, looking back on it, in comparison with, and viewed from a real concentration camp many of us found ourselves in later on, the ghetto had been sheer paradise.

I was fortunate in that in the room I shared with 6 other boys for a few months one of the boys was Paul Kling, a violin Wunderkind who had picked a good violin and a good bow from the lot offered by the Germans. As there had been no music at all in my life as we had to hand in radios, gramophones and records and entry to any public performance was prohibited to Jews as well, it was marvellous to be just a few feet away from him, due to the room being very crammed with 3-storey bunk beds, listening to the most intricate pieces played with the greatest of ease.

I then spent a few weeks in a children's hospital with suspected nephritis, inflammation of the kidneys, and, on being discharged, I was also moved to a different house with different boys but the love of classical music and some understanding of its technical aspects

have stayed with me. Paul survived Auschwitz and a slave labour camp, as well as a death march and became leader of orchestras in Tokyo, and Kentucky, ending his career as Professor of Music at the University of British Columbia at Vancouver.

Our stay came to an end on 12th October 1944 when my mother and I were put on one of 11 transports which emptied the ghetto of 18,402 people, or of about half of its population between 28th September and 28th October 1944. The Germans wanted to make full use of their Auschwitz gas chambers before they blew them up. 1,574 people were still alive on liberation, a death rate of 91.5%.

My father had been sent on 29 September 1944 on a transport of 1,500 people of whom 79 survived. He was not among them. Our transport was also made up of 1,500 people of whom 78 survived. My mother was not among them either. I am one of the 78 who survived from that transport.

We had travelled in a third class carriage with wooden slatted seats, not in a cattle truck like most other transports, it just depended on what the Czech and German railways had available. They got paid, as did the French and Dutch railways, for ferrying the condemned to their death and they knew perfectly well what they were doing. We travelled throughout the night, so there was nothing to see anyway, and we arrived in the morning of the 13th October 1944. We didn't know where we were, we had never seen anything like it, and it was confusing, alarming and frightening. We were ordered out of the carriage and had to leave our luggage behind, they were our last possessions which even those few who survived were never to see again. Robbing the Jews was as much on the German agenda as murdering them.

Orderlies, prisoners in striped prison uniform, which we had never encountered before, who had done this before many a time, put women and children into a queue six abreast, and men and boys into a second queue, parallel with the first.

I was a bit slow, or overwhelmed, but my mother spotted me, left her place in the queue, came over to me, shook me by the hand, and returned to her place. There was some sort of ramp at the end of which stood some SS men. The women, girls and babies went up the ramp first, one by one, as directed by the prisoner-orderlies. I saw my mother turn left at the end of the ramp.

The women were quickly disposed of, quite literally, then it was the men's and boys' turn and then my turn. I went up the ramp, not taking any notice of the men in their black uniform and turned to the left, to follow my mother. I was hauled back. Your fate was decided by the moving indicator finger of the senior SS officer, moving it to the right or to the left, it could have been Mengele. As I had taken no notice of the men, I had taken no notice of the finger of one of them but, obviously, a bystander had, that was probably his job, to make sure the decisions on life and death of the parade of the damned were carried out. I was turned to the right and joined a small group of men.

That encounter on the ramp was one of the links of a chain of events which caused me to survive and be here tonight. The selected few were marched away, taken to a large room where we had to undress, putting our clothes on one heap. That was the last time for a very long time that I had worn my own clothes. We had a short shower, all the hair on our bodies was shaved off using blunt razor blades. The hair on one's head was removed with clippers. Lice lay their eggs on hair, lice carry typhus bacteria, typhus is deadly, is no respecter of person, even the SS could get it. Hence all hair had to come off.

We were issued with new, or rather with very second, third or fourth-hand clothing, but not of the striped variety. My black jacket had a large red cross in dark red painted on its back, shoes were wooden clogs, and underpants were made from prayer shawls. Prayer shawls are made from best wool, as it was October in cold Poland; they did us a favour making us wear them. There were no vests or shirts, only thin brown blankets which we wrapped around us. The cap was important; you had to doff it with a flourish every time you saw a German guard appear.

We were taken to a wooden hut, one of many. They all looked the same and it was difficult to find the hut you had been allocated as all the inmates also looked the same. Our fate had been arranged before we had even left the ghetto. The manager of a firm, called VDM and still in existence, had the contract to produce propellers from aluminium castings for the German air force. He needed cheap labour to maximise profits. He was already using Czech and French forced labour but wanted something really cheap but intelligent and if they could speak German and there were a few professional engineers among them, a few doctors and maybe a mathematician, so much the better. Like any other German factory manager he requested Jewish slave labour from the administrators of Auschwitz. He was promised the survivors of the next transport from Theresienstadt, a ghetto which seems to have had the reputation of consisting of the intelligentsia, that was us. In the end there weren't enough survivors from our transport, but that is another story.

Not only were we told on the first night that we were very lucky because we were going to be sent to work somewhere with a roof over our heads and not in the open as were most of the others, but on the second night this manager came into our hut, a man in civilian clothing, a raincoat with the circular party member emblem in his lapel, and selected us by, once again, pointing his finger. If anybody ever tells you that the Germans didn't know what was going on you can tell them that not only did they know but that they actually entered Auschwitz and other camps and that Allianz insurance company agents inspected them because they insured them. He didn't stray far from the door to our hut because that open door provided light from the outside. The bulbs fitted to the concrete supports of the electrified barbed wire provided more light that the very weak bulbs inside the hut. I happened to stand near that door, he happened to see me, he pointed at me, and from that moment onwards I was one of his slave workers. On the 19th of October 1944 we were put on a train, in cattle trucks, standing room only, off to Friedland.

It was work in a factory, as we had been told, and we had a roof over our heads even if conditions were not exactly rosy. The 12-hour shifts were beyond our endurance for the little food we received and the work was quite hard. The propellers were made from aluminium but they were large and solid. Nevertheless it was better than working in the open at an aircraft fuel-from-coal plant, like Felix Weinberg, exposed to the elements and constant bombing by the 8th US Army Air Corps, not being allowed into shelters and likely to be hit by shrapnel from bombs as well as from falling anti-aircraft shells. It was another link in the chain.

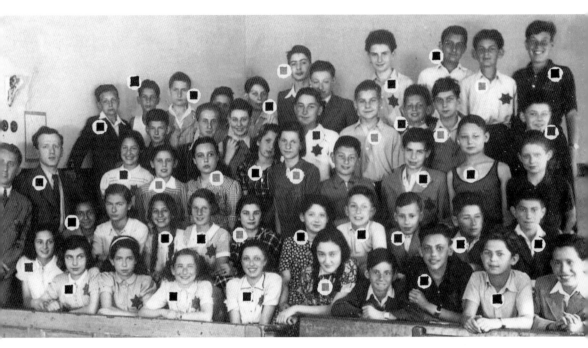

### Frank Bright's Classmates

*Class photo of class IIB of the Jewish school in Prague, taken shortly before the school was closed in June or July of 1942. It is not complete; by the time the photo was taken some of my classmates had already been deported. Those with a black square were murdered, those with a grey one survived till liberation.*

A classmate of mine from Prague happened to stand at the other end of the hut. He too had survived the selection at the ramp on arrival. The manager of the Friedland factory did not see him standing in the dark away from the door, did not point at him, and did not select him. He was sent somewhere else and died on the 3rd of January 1945 in Dachau of starvation in the arms of his younger brother. I traced the widow of that brother to Melbourne, Australia. I happened to be at the right spot at the right time. That was what one's fate depended on. Luck. Not on wanting to survive, everybody did that.

*A talk delivered by Frank Bright to the Suffolk Jewish Community on Friday, 2nd August 2013 in the Salvation Army Citadel, Ipswich.*

# Graham Locking:

## An interview with a Racing Chaplain

**As a chaplain, based in Newmarket, what is your exact role in horseracing?**

My role is to offer pastoral care and to support members of the racing community. That means helping them when there are problems and encouraging them in their daily lives. I am on the gallops every morning and go to the yards so that people are aware of me. I talk to trainers and visit stables, getting to know people and building relationships so that I can help if needed. Along with Racing Welfare and the Injured Jockeys Fund, I am always available. Instead of sitting in an office waiting for people to come to me I go out and meet them.

**Why did you get involved in the sport and what is the most rewarding aspect of your job?**

I got involved because my idea of what church is about – and it's not preaching in a building – it is relating to people. I started out working in the East End of London with homeless vagrants, alcoholics and drug addicts. I also set up a counselling centre in Sheffield and a neighbourhood youth play-centre in Birkenhead. I have always enjoyed working with people outside the church and when the advertisement for a chaplain to horseracing appeared in the religious press 12 years ago, I was immediately interested. My grandmother used to take me to our local track, Market Rasen, as a kid and I used to love watching racing on television.

The most rewarding part is being able to help people. I conducted Michael Jarvis's funeral in September and more recently did the tribute at the funeral of Robert Fellowes, who had been manager of Jockey Club Estates for 28 years. Another enriching experience was when a young girl at the British Racing School was going through a tough time. I was able to meet with her a couple of times and she is now a changed person.

*It is not my job to preach religion, it is to help people.*

## How do you balance religion with the unusual and, at times, eccentric world of horseracing?

For me, religion is a celebration of life; it is not about a restricted set of codes or practices. In all of that there are times when we do well and times when we don't do so well, and racing is part of that life. It is not my job to judge people or criticise. If racing is getting a bad press that's all the more reason I should be involved. That's when people, who are struggling under pressure, are inclined to do silly things and need support and encouragement.

## Can you get close to the trainers, jockeys and the stable staff?

We conducted a survey in 2009 and 87% of those surveyed in Newmarket knew me and over 91% of those I'd helped were more than satisfied. I was with Sir Henry Cecil when his brother David died and I am close to many of the trainers. I know the lads well, though staff does change all the time. If you show an interest in them and don't talk to them about God they will respond.

It is not my job to preach religion, it is to help people and if I am going to do that I need to know those concerned. Therefore, when I go round yards I chat to them generally, maybe about their mother, their granny, their wife, husband, partner, children, even their football team. One of my favourite sayings is: 'I share the love of God with people every day, but only very occasionally talk about it.' If I am going to care for people I must build relationships with them, not spew out a lot of religious claptrap.

## Have you been more in demand since the economic downturn took hold?

I think trainers are struggling and it is a time when people need more support. They need someone to blast off at, someone to listen to their problems. The middle and small trainers are all struggling, and they and their staff need someone to understand them. I am not a clever shit with all the answers because I haven't got the answers, but I can listen, sympathise and help. I realise they are going through tough times, though most won't admit it publicly.

## How big a problem is depression among racing employees?

About eight years ago in Newmarket we had three suicides all within about five weeks of each other and we got together Samaritans, a local drug rehabilitation unit, doctors and police to examine the question of drugs, alcohol and depression in horseracing. We discovered that racing does not have any more drug addicts, alcoholics or people suffering from depression than any other workforce. But we do have our fair share. Racing is inclined to be labelled as having more gamblers and ne'er-do-wells than other sports, but it is not true; there are lots of people in the industry who lead normal lives. I accept that depression in sport is a big issue. I have a colleague, who works in the Premier League, and he is trying to help footballers suffering from depression.

The most common problem with the people I come into contact with in racing is self-esteem. Sometimes they get into such a mess they don't believe in themselves. They come into racing with all the dreams in the world wanting to be jockeys, but the reality is most of them won't make it. But they should realise that riding out is as important as being a jockey; the stable lad rides the horse every morning, the jockey only occasionally. The trouble is stable staff have never been given the esteem or value they warrant as skilled people. So they become downcast and frust-rated, and that can be expressed in drug addiction and alcoholism, which they misguidedly believe is making them worth-while. Newmarket has a drug problem, but no worse than the average town.

**Do you ever get calls from trainers or jockeys when they are on a bad run?**

I don't have a lot of dealings with jockeys because they are always on the move and trainers won't come knocking on my door, but at times I can tell when some are having it tough. That's when I'll pop round to their yard. But it needs to be someone who knows me; they don't want some strange vicar poking his nose in. That's where the on-going relationship is vital. You never impose yourself, otherwise you'll be told to go forth and multiply. I have to admit there are one or two trainers I haven't spoken to apart from a good morning and goodbye, and that's fine by me.

**To what extent do you participate in the Newmarket scene?**

My involvement with Racing Welfare, the British Racing School and the Astley Club brings me close to much of the community. I organise, along with a group of women known as the 'Vic's Chicks', the Christmas Carol Concert at Tattersalls, where we have a congregation of 500 every year.

*Christianity is about caring for people and, therefore, has a place in racing*

**What do you enjoy most about living and working in Newmarket?**

Being on the gallops early in the morning is the most fantastic experience. First lot on Warren Hill, with the sun rising, you can watch 500 or 600 racehorses going about their training. Try and find me a better sight in the world. You won't.

**Is there one issue above all others that racing needs to address urgently?**

I never try to comment on racing politics because I don't have the knowledge. Obviously prize-money rears its head, and also the way we treat people is very important. When we had the controversial business in Newmarket about whether Lord Derby should build all those houses on the Hatchfield estate in town, Peter Stanley, Lord

Derby's brother and chairman of the Astley Club, and I were about the only two people in Newmarket who didn't have a view on the matter.

## What is your view on gambling and how do you reconcile betting with religion?

Gambling is like so many other things, enjoyable. We all know it is part of our industry but it is like alcohol and like driving a car, both enjoyable but highly dangerous when out of control. It is not a question of the actual gambling, it's the losing control – take a car at 90 mph and it is a danger; excessive alcohol or betting beyond one's means both cause anxiety and unhappiness. You find people trying to invest in gambling to make up for what they are missing in their lives – using gambling to make their lives meaningful and as a result becoming addicted. It's the misuse of gambling and alcohol that puts people in danger.

## Why aren't more vicars involved in horseracing? After all, Irish priests come in their droves to Cheltenham!

It is partly because the Irish racing fraternity have a mentality of a gathered community, meaning they are more together in their churches and with their fellow priests than we are. We have about 220 chaplains who visit football clubs and other sports. We have had a chaplaincy team at Ascot for the last five years; there are two chaplains on duty at most meetings and as many as four at the Royal meeting. A husband and wife were recently at Ascot when he collapsed with a heart attack and within minutes two chaplains were on hand to comfort the poor woman while her husband was fighting for his life.

## Should the church play a bigger part in the industry?

My thoughts are that we have something to offer at our best, though at our worst the church is intolerable. However, at our best we do care, we have skills and experience, and once you get beyond the vicar image then people do want to engage. In the right circumstances and with the right clergy we could play a bigger part in racing.

In a poll commissioned by Racing Welfare over 70% who responded to the questionnaire said chaplaincy in racing should be extended across the country. Recently I recorded a short piece for Channel 4's '4Thought', which will be screened immediately after the Channel 4 news sometime in July. I explain that religion is part of life, racing is part of life, and that Christianity is about caring for people and, therefore, has a place in racing.

**Do other training centres have their own chaplains?**

Recently I met the local clergy in Malton and Norton and talked to them about making monthly visits to yards to offer pastoral care, advice and support. We are in the process of contacting trainers in the area prepared to help us develop our plans. We have had an ongoing relationship with Lambourn but their clergy keeps changing. Sometimes church people become very huddled together within their churches and part of my task is to try to inspire them to get involved in the racing community.

**How does life in Newmarket compare with having a pastoral flock?**

I had a pastoral flock for 22 years and now it is so freeing to be with people who have no pre-conceived ideas about God or vicars. I can relate to people just as they are. So I don't have to worry about offending people because we haven't chosen this hymn or that prayer. I don't have to wrestle with church politics anymore because I don't have my own church.

**Do you ever bet or get lots of tips?**

I have had five bets in my 12 years at Newmarket and, would you believe, they have all won. You see, I take advice: there's no point in being special adviser to the stars if you're not going to take advantage of it!

*Taken from 'Thoroughbred Owner & Breeder incorporating Pacemake'*
*The official magazine of the Racehorse Owners' Association and*
*Thoroughbred Breeders' Association.*

# Gudrun Warren: My German Daddy

When you are little, whatever you know is what is "normal". I couldn't understand how my schoolfriends could leave a letter for Father Christmas on Christmas Eve and still get what they wanted for Christmas, because we left letters in a Wellington boot on the stairs on St Nicholas' Day (6 December). This, of course, left plenty of shopping days to Christmas…

Why did we follow this practice? Because Daddy was German. We didn't speak German, but we were "the cousins with the funny names". Mother was one of four in the class with the same name, and vowed her children wouldn't suffer that, so Daddy produced a list of names, and she chose the one she liked best.

We didn't talk much about this at home. To mark the fortieth anniversary of D-Day I was asked to talk to a relative who had a memory of the Second World War, and to learn from them a war song. I talked to my aunt (wife of my mother's brother), and my song was "There'll be blue birds over the white cliffs of Dover". Princess Michael of Kent was in the news at about this time, because her father had been "outed" as an SS officer. I lived in daily dread of something similar happening to my father: because I didn't really know much about his history, I didn't know whether he, too, might have been an SS officer.

He wasn't. He was in the infantry. He had wanted to be a police officer, but by the time he was old enough (and tall enough) to apply to the police force, you were required also to be a member of the SS. So that ended that ambition.

Throughout the time I shared with him, he suffered from terrible chilblains. He had served on the Russian Front. He had been badly frostbitten, and the chilblains were a legacy of that damage.

My mother is a devout church-goer, Church of England. My father was actually Lutheran, but came to the parish church on three occasions in the year: Christmas, Easter, and – he had grown up on a farm – Harvest Thanksgiving.

As a child, one of the most challenging days of my year was Remembrance Sunday; it still is, but not in quite the way it was. We gathered around the town war memorial and prayed for "our glorious dead". As far as I am aware, none of my close ancestors were killed in fighting in either war, but I knew some stories of involvement in action: one grandfather, a merchant seaman, had been involved in the evacuation of the Normandy beaches; the other, wounded on the Western Front, was not found until gangrene had taken hold to the extent that his leg had to be amputated. One was English, the other German. I looked at the War Memorial; I listened to the prayers for those who had died that we might be free.

I respect those who have died or been injured in the service of their country. But that extends to both sides. Who are we to judge why people fight for their country? Did all those conscripted in England deserve to be considered pure victims, almost martyrs? Did all those conscripted in Germany deserve to be considered inhumane and capable of despicable atrocities? My father didn't want to fight. He escaped drafting through being a farmer, a position held, in the English phrase, as a "reserved occupation". But when he was called up, what would you expect him to do? I have had held before me the examples of people such as Dietrich Bonhoeffer, who refused to be drawn into Hitler's service. I have felt that people are therefore labelling my father as a coward, or a Nazi sympathizer, a murderer.

But surely he was just an ordinary young man, full of the same contradictions as an English twenty-year-old: subject to the emotional blackmail that if you didn't join up you weren't a worthy son of your country; scared? not wanting to be sent away from family and loved ones; not wanting to die fighting many miles from home, part of a war machine that is so much greater than you. The English don't have to deal with that issue: the English won, and history, as we know well, is written by the victors, so the English have fixed it that the English men were all heroes, by the Second World War, at any rate; the families of shellshock victims of the Great War, executed for cowardice, might find themselves in a similar mental strife to mine.

Now, older, and what seems like many years further distanced from the war, I don't perhaps struggle as I used to with this... split loyalty? No – I feel no loyalty to Hitler's Germany, nor even to today's Germany. What I learnt as a child, though was that all men are related as children of God; all those who died left loved ones behind to grieve their loss; all "ordinary" people are caught up in the machinations of politicians, to which they can only respond as seems right and feasible to them at that time.

# Gurmeet Singh Sually:

## Perspective of a young Sikh

My name is Gurmeet Singh Sually. I am 20 years old and I am a practising Sikh.

If you ask me "What does Sikhism mean to you?" I have to say first that there are many different viewpoints and beliefs within the Sikh community not only nationally but also internationally.

For me, firstly, as a practising Sikh, the main points of reference are: the Guru Granth Sahib (Sikh scriptures) and the Dasam Granth (a separate book ascribed to Guru Gobind Sikh and/or his poets). The key generic beliefs in Sikhism are as follows:

- God is One and is the Creator of all things.
- All human beings are equal in God's sight.
Basic principles for living as a Sikh include:
- Pure vegetarianism – no eggs, no meat, no fish (and no other animal products),
- Teetotalism, so definitely no alcohol,
- No smoking or illegal drug use,
- Uncut hair.

These few beliefs above are truly the bedrock principles of Sikhism, especially in the 21st century.

As a young person and like many other young Sikhs, I see a clear difference between religious and spiritual learning and understanding compared to historic political discourse. The whos, whys and whens of Sikh history are very important and have their place; however, they should not compromise the messages and day-to-day practices of a Sikh.

Sikhism in its entirety is and should be understood in its simplest form. Basically this means applying the teachings of the Gurus from the scriptures to day-to-day living. A key theme and fundamental concept in Sikhism is to be a better human being, not just for your own benefit but also for those around you, such as family and friends.

Humility, kindness and Seva are and should be a few of the characteristics of Sikhs. Seva translates in English to selfless service, but the concept of Seva can be misinterpreted greatly. This fundamental belief is, in a way, the DNA of Sikhism.

The place of worship for Sikhs is the Gurdwara and this is where Seva begins to become more profound and is given much clearer understanding. A Gurdwara is a place that serves its community, regardless of an individual's race, religion, hair colour, political beliefs etc.

The basic rules when in a Gurdwara are, remove shoes upon entrance, wash hands and cover head before entering either the prayer room or the langar hall (food hall). Depending on the location of the Gurdwara, meaning town, city or country, some things may vary; however the following are universal.

There will be a large functional kitchen to make pure vegetarian food. There will be a langar hall, where the community can eat and of course a prayer room, usually situated upstairs. In India for instance, some Gurdwaras also have large rooms for people to rest or sleep, areas for people to work or study, a pharmacy or even an area for medical attention. These things all vary depending on the size and the location of the Gurdwara.

However, we must not portray the Gurdwara as a Sikh temple, for in its pure translation it is the "door to The Lord" (gur from the word Guru, meaning teacher, and dwara, meaning door). This deeper meaning reflects the clear message of Guru Ram Das who gave the name Gurdwara to emphasise equality amongst people, not to create segregation within a multicultural country. This is a key example of how Sikh history and spiritual practices work together.

Having a solid understanding of these things above allows us to build a stronger foundation for both our individual spirituality and also that of the wider sangat (sangat = community).

I sometimes attend the Gurdwara in Ipswich, however, more often than not, we attend the Gurdwara in London, where my grandmother and most of my family live, or in Leicester where my brother lives. In these big cities Gurdwaras are open all the time and are rarely closed. In Ipswich the Sikh community is quite small, but because of the Internet I am able to keep in touch with the wider Sikh community nationally and internationally. I spend a lot of time on Facebook, which has a page focused on topical Sikh issues for young Sikhs. This is called the Sikh Youth Project.

Equality does not just surround gender and age but especially today sexual orientation is a hot topic. As a young Sikh today, from my understanding as a Sikh, a core belief is that God has created everything and everyone exactly how he wishes them to be. We as human beings do not have the right to judge others or to question the Creator's grand design.

People are very surprised when they find out that my father is a Sikh and my mother is a Hindu. They married each other regardless of their respective faiths and despite their different backgrounds; even at the time in the mid '80s when there were strong social conflicts due to the then prime ministers, and exacerbated by Indira Gandhi's assassination.

As a result of my upbringing I can respect and understand people of many different backgrounds, and am comfortable in any place of worship.

# Heather Bruce: Why I joined the Quakers

I came to attend a Quaker meeting through practising Buddhist Meditation. I found meditation to be an important part of my spiritual development as it helped me develop a connection with my inner self and to consider more the wider community with love and compassion.

I happened to pass by the Ipswich Quaker Meeting House one Sunday and noticed on a poster that Quakers met in silence. I decided to enter to sit in meditation and experience the silence the Quaker Meeting had to offer. In this meeting I found a group of people open minded towards individuals beliefs, regardless of how different they may be to their own. I have found I cannot commit myself to any one singular religious teaching or spiritual path, as I felt sure others paths had been laid that led to the same Truth I seek.

My spiritual life or current path does not include God as my understanding of existence has to include no one literal answer or translation or explanation to this place I have a life in. It is a relief for me to have found some individuals in Ipswich meeting, who on their own spiritual or religious paths, also do not like the word God or the word religious for that matter.

Out of all the variety of practices Quakers have, both traditional and newly adopted, two things lead me to know that Quakerism was right for me. One was the recognition that Quakers are known for their activism; speaking truth to power. The second I discovered in a box in the meetinghouse library, a poster that states "Thou shalt decide for yourself. No one telling you what to believe, just the peace and quiet to work it out for yourself." This openness above everything else helped me to decide Ipswich meeting was to be my spiritual home.

Part of being a Quaker asks one to hold the Quaker Testimonies as guides. These testimonies do not encroach or contradict any part of the spiritual path I am following. I find in them a guide which is in tune with my natural way of being. The testimonies are to Simplicity, Truth,

Peace and Equality. In simplicity I find a less consumerist orientated way of living which aligns to my views towards the suffering of all that lives on our planet. In Truth I have found solid ground to hold to; seeking the Truth in existence. In Peace I found an action that is challenging to life's daily predation, whilst Equality is the testimony that resonates most closely with myself at present. In this testimony I find strength and challenges in treating all of life equally. The Mystics tell us we are all one and have to lose ourselves to find our true nature. I find equality to be the central part of my path.

I believe by considering what the testimonies speak of and working within a type of Quaker decision-making (known as discernment) that Quakers achieve their aims and act in a way that is a positive force in the world.

# Irmild Jacyna: Refugees – 1944

The first recollections I have are of summer 1944. We had to leave our home in Königsberg, Prussia, now Kaliningrad. We went to live on the farm in my mother's home in Loetzen, Prussia, the Land of the Thousand Seas. In August 1944 most of Königsberg was destroyed by two days of heavy bombing. The town burned for several weeks as most people had the winter supplies of coal in their cellars. In the winter we had to move again; the Russians were coming closer to the lovely peaceful countryside.

The farmers loaded what they could on the wagons pulled by horses and headed towards the west. We were asked to travel with my aunty and uncle and their three children. My uncle was still a farmer not a soldier. But my mother thought we would travel faster on foot when all the people left and the roads were blocked. It would also be safer as we could take cover quicker when the planes came again. It was lucky for us that we did not travel with our relations. My little cousin of about my age had both legs blown off by a grenade. She died before they could reach a hospital.

My mother packed a small suitcase with just one change of clothes for my sister, aged three and a half, for myself, aged five and a half, and for herself, with our birth certificates and the Bible. We had a sleigh and mother pulled us. We were wrapped in blankets as it was very cold. We travelled like this for days, passing most of the wagons on the way. It was a very cold winter with a lot of snow. A train took us some way and our sleigh was thrown out of the window to make room for just one more person. It was so crowded that some children had to sit over seats with the luggage. We were bombed by the British and Americans and could hear the guns of the Russians.

About Christmas time we arrived in Braunsberg. We were trying to get to Danzig (now Gdansk). There was a short cut over the Frisches Haff, so we went with the trek and all the other refugees over the frozen sea. It was heavy going since my mother had the two of us and the small suitcase. Sometimes we would have a ride on a wagon for a bit, that is until the next bombing. The planes came very low and we were shot at by the British and Americans. We were told not to pick up anything like pens, dolls, or little toys. They had been dropped by the Americans and were filled with explosives. When they got warm they would explode and blow a child's hands off. We had seen a few. My little sister had great fun watching the planes firing at us as she liked the flashing lights. She was too young to realise what it was. We walked like this for many days. It was hard going. At night we slept under some wagon on the ice.

One day I noticed a pram with a baby. It was crying and its mother lay, shot dead, next to the pram. I asked my mother if we could take the baby with us. She started to cry and said that she had got enough to struggle with to get us to safety. Looking back I can see that now; but I often wonder what happened to that child. Did someone save it or did it go down and drown in the pram?

We saw so many people shot or wounded. When a bomb cracked the ice we saw the sea open up in front of us and the horses and wagons and everything else on it going down. The crying; the noise of the horses; the wagons; the planes and the bombs; these are things I shall never forget. (I am still scared of planes, especially at night).

When we finally arrived in Danzig, we had to sleep on the floor in a church for some time. It was very cold. Then we were taken to a big house. Only the owner was still there. His wife and children had fled to the west. Now we could sleep in beds again after weeks on the road, have a bath and wash our clothing. We could treat the house like our home. In the cellar there were boxes of toys. We were allowed to play with them but we always put them back in the boxes later.

One day there was an air raid. We were taken to the cellar, but I went back upstairs to fetch my doll. The house was hit. My mother and the owner came looking for me. I stood in the corner of the room, my mother in the hallway, between us a big hole. Planks of wood were put across to get me to safety.

Some weeks later we were told we could get by ship to Denmark. There were no more trains going to the west. The Russians were only a few miles away. Only women with children and the old would be allowed to go. My mother became friendly with an old couple and their adult daughter. The couple got tickets to go but not their daughter, so my mother let one of us go with the lady, so that she would be able to leave with her parents. Luckily, we all went together.

Then the day arrived when we went to the docks. Six boats were there to take the refugees. First we went on a boat called 'Gunslow'. As we were boarding it we met our dentist and spoke to him. He waved goodbye to us but we were sent off the boat as it was overloaded. We had to board another boat. After sailing, we were bombed. The Gunslow was hit and went down with only a few people surviving. None of the other boats could pick anybody up as they were all overloaded. We were on deck and heard the screaming and crying for help. It was terrible. Even though I was so young it will always stay with me.

When we arrived in Denmark we lived first in a big school in Copenhagen. We all slept on the floor. Next to me slept an old man. He used to be a teacher so he started classes for the children. There was also a class for adults to learn English. My mother was one of the students. Like most of the children there, we had the whooping cough. The school had very high walls, but sometimes my sister and I were allowed to go out and mix with the Danish children. One of them was Princess Margaretha, now the Queen of Denmark. The nice guard would also take us to the baker's shop.

After six months in Copenhagen we had to go to a refugee camp near Aalberg. But I refused to go, since I had an older sister. When we left Konigsberg I was told she was in hospital and would follow when she was better. But up until then she had not come. I was not leaving again as I was afraid she would not find us. Now my mother had to tell me that my sister had died before we left. She had heart trouble. As I had the same heart condition, my mother kept it from me. We were very close and so she was worried that I would also die. After hearing that, I was ill for a long time.

My mother was a cook before she married. After we came to the camp she became a cook there which meant that sometimes we had a bit more food. We had very little food, hardly any vegetables, very rarely meat, and only horse meat. Some women had between the barracks little gardens where they grew onions, carrots and herbs. We had very few clothes and one silver teaspoon. We had taken the spoon from the house in Danzig. My mother used it for cooking and all three of us ate with it. It is now my treasure.

The winter of 1946-1947 was very hard. At one time the snow was so deep that only the chimneys were visible from the air. We pushed the snow to the side and made a tunnel to the next barrack. All the others did the same so we were all connected. We heated the barracks with wood which was rationed. As it was so very cold my mother arranged with some other women from our barrack to fell a tree at night. They cut the tree into logs about 30 cm long, which were hidden under the head-ends of our beds. We all had a log as they had to dry before we could burn them. It was soon discovered that a tree had been felled and they searched for the wood but could not find it. We would have been in trouble had they discovered who was responsible.

In June 1947, we were told we could go back to Germany. The Red Cross had found my father near Frankfurt am Main. He had got married just before. He had met our dentist who had seen us go onto the boat, the Gunslow, so he believed we had drowned. When he first saw us again he did not know that his eldest daughter had died, age 9, in Konigsberg. He had only seen me a few times, and had not seen my youngest sister. Now she was 6 years old and I was 8. We went to live in a small village where most of the people were Catholic. We had a very hard time at school as we were among the few who were Protestant. But worst of all we were unwanted refugees, Germans, but outsiders.

I don't know how my mother had the courage and faith to come through all this. I only saw her cry a few times. Once was when she had to refuse me taking that baby in the pram. The other time was when I was so hungry that my tummy hurt and I asked her for some food and she had none. I never asked again. She used to cook nettles (they were like spinach) and potato peelings from the others who were better off. We collected rosehips, cleaned them out and cooked them so we would get vitamins. I never knew where she got all this from or how to do it. For seven years we lived, slept, washed and cooked in one room of about 10-12 feet until in 1954 my mother died of cancer. We were up until then brought up with so much love. We were very close, the three of us. My father stayed with his second wife, even though the marriage was not legal. But they had a house, an electrical shop and two apprentices, also a child and later on two more. Every evening we went for walks, my mother would talk of home and dream of the day we would return. At dusk we would go home. We drank cocoa while my mother read the Bible to us; in the seven years she went through it two and a half times. She was a remarkable woman, they all liked her.

When I go on holiday there, more than 40 years later, the older people still remember her and say that mother was a lady. We were poor but at the end well liked. She helped so many. Our vicar (we were German Lutherans) was a great friend and regular guest in our home. He confirmed me in April 1954 and buried my mother in June 1954.

Now, 50 years since I left Königsberg, I have got a pen friend there, a Russian. He kindly sent me photographs of our house; it is one of the few still standing; 90% were destroyed. Also our church where we were baptised and which we attended still stands. The Russians use it as a cinema. The organ plays hit songs now, not hymns. But hopefully one day it will be used for worship again. We still hope that one day Königsberg will belong to Germany again. It was a seat for our kings for 700 years.

*first published in Finding our Way and Sharing our Stories (SIFRE 1994)*

# Isabelle Wen:

## A member of the Buddhist Community of Interbeing

I was born in Norwich of a French mother and English father. After graduating from university I spent 6 years in China teaching English and studying acupuncture. I only had a very vague interest in Buddhism then but I suppose I started to get my head around the Asiatic way of looking at things.

My first contact with the Buddhist tradition of Thich Nhat Hanh's was a Day of Mindfulness organised by SIFRE at the Friends Meeting House in Ipswich, probably in the late 1990s. Then in 2001 I went with my two daughters (then 7 and 9), to Plum Village, Thich Nhat Hanh's monastic community in the south-west of France. We all had a fantastic time and I found my spiritual home. There happened to be 5 people from Ipswich there that summer and we have continued to meditate together every week since then.

We now form the Ipswich Sangha of the Community of Interbeing which is the national organisation of people practising in the tradition of Thich Nhat Hanh in the UK. We have several offshoot sanghas in different parts of Suffolk including Dunwich and Lawshall near Bury St Edmunds.

In 1997 I became a member of Thich Nhat Hanh's lay Order of Interbeing which entails a commitment to practice 14 Mindfulness Trainings, to represent Thich Nhat Hanh's tradition in this country and to help build the sangha. We organise national and regional retreats attended by Thich Nhat Hanh, other monastics and Dharma Teachers, amongst other activities.

Buddhism is not so much a religion for me as a practice. Beliefs don't play a large role, and in fact we are strongly encouraged not to take anything on trust but to test out all principles in our own lives, and especially not to try to force them on anyone else.

Thich Nhat Hanh's teachings are eminently practical. Mindfulness is his core practice. Mindfulness leads me to a better understanding of myself, and therefore everything around me including other people. When I can see a situation clearly it's much easier to see the solutions to problems. It's all about keeping it real, that is, seeing reality for what it really is.

Mindfulness of the breath is particularly helpful for the body and mind, and is the basis of most meditation techniques.

My daily meditation practice (supported by regularly attending the sangha) helps to keep me calm, grounded and resilient in times of stress. I'm so lucky that Thich Nhat Hanh also very much emphasises the importance of sowing the seeds of mindfulness in children and young people so that now the practices are helping my daughters in the difficult process of growing up.

Now that my daughters have both left home I have more time to help teach these wonderful tools to other children by organising family retreats and visiting local schools to talk about Buddhism and mindfulness.

By starting the process of watering the seeds of peace in myself I can see the effect on everything and everyone around me: a wonderful manifestation of Interbeing, another core Buddhist concept (we are all so interconnected that there is actually no separation between us).

# Janus van Helvert: How come I'm a Buddhist?

## Some background

Don't be fooled by my name, I'm a Suffolk man; this has always been my home. I was born in 1961 to working class parents, coming into the world in the bedroom of our council house. Children have been described as the flowers of their culture, so I guess I was a flower of the 'Spirit of '45', the post-war Labour landslide that created the NHS, built our solid home with its sizeable garden on Ipswich's Chantry estate, and gave me a good education. The jewel of education was planted by two primary school teachers, Mrs Massey and Mr Grimwood; it's been a pillar of my life – I went on to University, ultimately gaining six HE awards in very different subjects.

In my teens I saw the film Akenfield. Its portrait of village life, rooted and entwined in this Suffolk landscape, had a profound impact on me and illustrates a second pillar of my life – a deep connection to nature. I spent twenty years of my adult life in Suffolk villages, six of these living in an organic farming community; I'm a life member of the Soil Association and believe industrial farming to be a grave, inhumane error which will come back to bite us all. I'm a committed environmentalist and work in this field, formerly for Friends of the Earth, latterly for local government. I've been a Morris dancer for 22 years; the dance and music is for me, not only performance and community, but also a spiritual practice in its own way, that helps connect me to land and life.

And a third pillar, my wife and family; a daughter, two sons, a stepdaughter, a grandson, and a granddaughter arriving in a month's time.

## So how come I'm a Buddhist?

There's a quote in the documentary film 'An Ecology of Mind', "You might think you're thinking your own thoughts; you're not, you're thinking your culture's thoughts. The major problems in the world result from the difference between how nature works and how people think. What does it even mean to change the way we think?"

Through my 20s I became aware I'd been socialised into my culture's Western Enlightenment way of thinking, and that despite its technological achievements, this thinking had some serious limitations. Its machine metaphor, reductionism and dualism offered me no profound insight into the nature of life, consciousness and meaning. And its materialist ideologies (communism, capitalism) seemed to cause as much if not more inhumanity and suffering than any that went before. The crisis in Western Enlightenment civilisation and thinking is well illustrated I feel by its impotence in addressing two problems that threaten our very existence: environmental degradation and nuclear weapons. Stephan Harding's **'Animate Earth'** and Rupert Sheldrake's **'The Science Delusion'** are recent books exploring some of these issues.

Western religion, with its creator god and a deified Jesus, failed to address these issues for me, in fact seemed to be the seed of the enlightenment cul-de-sac. I was drawn instead to eastern philosophies, particularly Buddhism, but many Buddhist writings seemed to have a tendency toward nihilism and escapism. Then, through my second wife, I found the writings of Daisaku Ikeda and the SGI movement that had grown around the world under Ikeda's leadership. I've been a member of this movement now for 20 yrs.

**What has Nichiren Buddhism and the SGI given me?**

I've found not only a profound philosophy which addresses the issues I mentioned above, but also a daily practice chanting "nam myoho renge kyo" that helps develop inner strength, courage, wisdom and compassion to embrace others. It's not some magic panacea but a tool to use in our continuing struggle to create meaning and value in our lives, breaking through our delusions, anguish, fear, lack of self-worth and depression. Some days I win, some days I lose, but the teachings and practice I've found, and the support of my faith community, are treasures in my life.

I'd been working in ICT for a number of years when I met the practice (initially in the city, then in local government). My Buddhist practice helped me develop the courage to change direction, initially into teaching and then into the environmental field. In my personal life it has helped me develop deep respect for my first wife, despite the differences that led us to part, as we continued to share the upbringing of our two children. It also helped me in my step parenting and helped me cherish and support my mother during her final years. And last but not least, coming back to my name, my practice has helped me transform my experience with my father, as follows.

## Deeply appreciating my heritage

For my first eleven years Dad was the most important person in my life; then he was gone; heart disease through smoking too much. It wasn't just the pain of his loss but also not having him around to help me explore who I was that used to cause me great suffering. He's been dead 40 years but my relationship with him has continued as I've explored the ancestry he gave me and learnt more about the events that shaped his life.

Dad was born and grew up in Suriname when it was a Dutch colony. It's in the tropics on the South American mainland and has a Caribbean culture. His father (my namesake) was Dutch. His mother was Creole, relatively light-skinned since her father was a poor German immigrant and her maternal grandfather a Dutch Jewish immigrant. She was the daughter of a woman born into slavery who became free as a child following abolition. My twin half-sisters, my cousins and I, are the first generation of our grandmother's line to be entirely white.

My dad was drafted into the Dutch army at the start of WW2, fought from Suffolk and settled here. He helped liberate his father's home town, won the Netherlands' highest award for bravery, had his left leg blown off two days before the war ended, suffered post-traumatic stress which saw him attempt suicide and led to the failure of his first marriage. My twin half-sisters grew up in the States; I was 30 and they were 44 when we first met. Dad won through though; worked on building sites as a painter and decorator for 20 years, despite having only one leg, married my mother, was a good father to me, but couldn't give up the fags; he needed them to hold it together.

I've come to realise that not only my father's ancestry, but also his premature death, was a great gift. It's driven me to understand my personal and our collective history. I'm the son of an immigrant; I'm a mongrel, personally connected to issues like colonialism, slavery, racism, the fight against fascist thinking, and the horrors of war. This has opened up my heart and mind to many things.

## Twelve million very different individuals, one common cause

I've shared this picture of me, a Buddhist here in Suffolk, to help dispel any stereotypes people may have. I suppose those who read it might now think all SGI members are just like me, but we're actually a very mixed bunch. There are a few famous names – Orlando Bloom, Howard Jones, Sandie Shaw, Roberto Baggio – but for the most part we're pretty normal!

The SGI movement has around 50 members in Suffolk, 11,000 across the UK from all walks of life and all ethnic groups, 100,000 across Europe and 12 million worldwide. We're ordinary people living alongside everyone else in communities and countries around the world (see: **www.sgi.org** and **www.sgi-uk.org** for more info); there's nothing that particularly marks us out.

Ikeda is in his 80s now and has led an amazing value creating life. He is our inspiration and our mentor. You might not have heard of him (see: **www.daisakuikeda.org** for more info) but to illustrate the esteem in which his accomplishments are held around the world, the university attended by Martin Luther King, when creating an award to honour King, eventually settled on calling it the Gandhi, King, Ikeda award.

The heart of our faith is belief in, and respect for, all life. This includes respecting freedom of thought, religious freedom, and a commitment to dialogue (these values are written into our constitution).

# Jean Gittens:

## A chat with a Seventh Day Adventist

At the SIFRE Seniors' monthly tea party, Jean spoke briefly about her experiences of coming to Ipswich from Barbados. She travelled to England in 1962 by plane to join her husband. He had arrived in 1960 and then sent for Jean. The first place they lived in had nine rooms and nine families living in them. Jean explained that she had to leave her children behind when she first came to England and that her aunt looked after them. This was not unusual in those days and indeed in England there was also the tradition of the extended family supporting its members. This does not happen so much now that more families are living apart from each other.

Jan Lelijveld asked Jean how long she had intended to come to England for and she said that the plan was that they would stay for five years, but by the time the children also came to England she was putting roots down. Jean pointed out, however, that if her mother had lived longer she would probably not be living in England now.

When she first came to this country Jean was anxious about getting a job. In fact she got one at the Suffolk Iron Foundry where lawn mowers were made. She was able to travel to work every day with other employees on her husband's minibus as he was also employed there. Once she had all her children with her she stopped at home with them and she did not go back to work until the youngest, Jessie, was three years old. After that she worked at the Ipswich Hospital as a nursing assistant until she retired.

In those days it was not always easy for immigrants to find a place of worship where they were accepted. However, Jean and her family were able to continue as Seventh Day Adventists as they were welcomed into the 7DA Church in Ipswich where she became an elder. Over the years Jean was involved in various courses and community events where she met women from other religious and cultural backgrounds and became firm friends with them. These friendships have been very valuable to her. Jean said that Ipswich had always been multi-cultural. There has been more silliness than real racism. Jean said she used to help out in the children's school and this also has helped her involvement in the local community.

Jean said that everyone knows her in her neighbourhood and that whenever anyone new moves into the area she always drops a note and leaves flowers for them and the note gives her address and says "I am Jean and we look out for each other in this neighbourhood."

# Jim Corrigall:

## My Christian Faith: Arriving late

Faith is a quality I discovered late in life, and I've considered myself a Christian now for just seven or eight years, since 2006.

I was born and brought up in South Africa, in a household with a strong commitment to social justice but without religious belief. After my father died, I was sent to an Anglican boarding school for secondary education, where I was baptised and confirmed in the Anglican faith. However, by the time I left school I considered myself an atheist and this was to remain my position for most of adulthood – despite developing a lifelong love of religious poetry at university.

My career was in journalism, which I pursued in South Africa (briefly), and then in Britain for most of my working life, with a spell in Zimbabwe during the 1980s. My final 17 years as a journalist were spent at BBC World Service in London, and I took early retirement from this job in 2007. Throughout my time in journalism, I was also active in struggles for social justice, in the anti-apartheid cause, and then as a trade unionist.

At the start of the new millennium, in the early 2000s, I began to feel the need for a deeper purpose to life. I greatly appreciated my family, my job at the BBC and work as a trade unionist – but I was increasingly wondering whether there was anything more to life. What was the purpose of it all? Was there any greater purpose?

I began to feel the need to explore my spirituality, and this led to a quest which saw me join the Unitarians in Britain in 2003. I was delighted to discover a religion that welcomed me as an agnostic and a seeker (as I then was), and which encouraged me to explore spirituality – which I did with enthusiasm.

However, after about two years, I began to feel the need for something deeper; could it be God? I tried Sufism for a while but was not sure if it was right for me. I recalled the words of the Dalai Lama, asked by an American seeker who sought the "Ultimate Reality", "Should I become a Buddhist?" The Dalai Lama replied firmly, "No, you should become a Christian." In fact, mystics of the East often so challenge Westerners seeking to embrace Hinduism or Buddhism, "Have you explored your own faith? The faith of your upbringing, of your people, of your culture? Perhaps you should try that, rather than the exotic?"

So I began to explore Christianity, and – in the writings of the Radical Reformation, in particular in mystics such as Boehme and Ruysbroek – I found a depth that drew me in. But I was finding belief very difficult – eventually though, through modern theologians like Marcus Borg and the 20th Century mystics Evelyn Underhill and Thomas Merton, I began to understand God not as something "out there", but more as the force, or spirit, that is both within and without, yet a spirit that is forever a mystery to us.

I was now reading the Bible regularly, and finding in its pages deep truths, truths that helped me make sense of life. I began to regard myself as a liberal Christian, and joined the Unitarian Christian Association, the body which aims "to preserve and strengthen" the liberal Christian tradition within the General Assembly of Unitarian and Free Christian Churches (the full name of the denomination in Britain).

My life since this time has – I hope – been one of deepening faith. After finding difficulty with regular prayer, I came across Ignatian spirituality – the mystical path developed by the founder of the Jesuits, Ignatius of Loyola, in the 16th century. I studied the Ignatian spiritual exercises with the Jesuits in central London for a year.

The Jesuits were very liberal; their advice was that only two things are needed to undertake the exercises. First, a concept of God (even if only seen as something within oneself), and second, an ability to work with metaphor (particularly of the Trinity). I found I was able to work with these, but I was also to find that the metaphors began to take on a life of their own.

For this reason, I've increasingly come to see myself as a Free Christian rather than a Unitarian Christian. Who are the Free Christians? They are our oldest tradition, those who seek to bring together *all* Christians: Unitarians, Trinitarians and those rejecting such labels, in a non-denominational Free Christian Church, a church open to all. They can also be called "Non-Subscribers"; those who believe that neither members nor ministers should be required to subscribe to creeds or statements of faith – they are those who respect private judgement in matters of faith.

My faith has helped me in many ways since 2006, including the inspiration to train as a Unitarian and Free Christian Minister. I completed my training in July 2012, and have subsequently served as Minister at Ipswich and Framlingham in Suffolk, which has been a great privilege.

I view faith as a journey and not as a destination – the journey continues, and I do not know the destination. But I hope and pray that God will continue to guide me and inspire me, along all my ways.

# Jnanamitra Emmett:

# On being a Transsexual and Buddhist

Two shaven headed men wearing colourful yellow robes, draped to their toes, walk mindfully down ancient steps, along a path made from large worn stones, and enter a huge wooden building with curved gables and heavily carved eaves. Taking their shoes off at the entrance they enter the dark interior where sounds of deep male voices can be heard chanting something mysterious and unintelligible. The camera pulls back revealing the building in its landscape of steep woods and mountains, threads of mist giving depth and mystery to the scene. The leaves of the trees are touched by autumn colours.

She leans back in the sofa laughing to her friends and presses STOP and EJECT. "If only it was as simple as it looks in a Kung Fu movie!" she says, "How can we convey the experience of what we Buddhists are without having to explain everything?" The question is met by smiles and nodding of heads, because she spends hours every week doing just that, talking to people who have come to her meditation class about what meditation really is, and how it can be done by ordinary people, in casual clothes, in our ordinary homes in our towns in the UK today by anyone who is willing to learn and to practice, never mind in misty temples, which are for men only, far far away.

Those people coming to the meditation class do not realise that she is a post-op male-to-female transsexual, not that there is any real risk of the kind of violence we see in the film 'Boys Don't Cry' about the short life of female-to-male transsexual Brandon, as 'he' mixes going out dressed as a man (whilst still having an untreated female form beneath), with being sexually active picking up women and acting rough and tough with the lads, amidst much beer and fags in redneck boondocks USA, with fatal consequences.

In contrast the Buddhist community we find here is relatively civilised, non-violent, alcohol free and kindly. Everyone who has become more seriously involved knows that she is TS, but that knowledge is part of knowing her well, and the core of the community have known her all through the process, and are familiar with it to the point of boredom. I will now let her tell her story.

I remember a time when I wasn't Buddhist (I had a middle class English Church of England upbringing), and I really hoped I wasn't transsexual, but that's a long time ago and you can read it in my book, when I write it. Back then I was interested in learning to meditate because I thought that, if I was able to concentrate more easily, I would be more effective in my life. At the same time I was opening up to my transsexualism by attending a self-help group in Islington, London. I saw them as two quite different things.

The Buddhism I encountered was a second-generation form led by an Englishman who had been a monk in India for 20 years and who has really tried to pare away the cultural accretions of the centuries so that modern Westerners could engage with Buddhist practice in a way that is relevant to our lifestyle, culture and experience. But that didn't mean that the movement he started was ready for the modern West in the form of a transsexual.

I like Buddhism because it is relatively free of beliefs, it is very pragmatic and practical; it involves doing things, practising. It says you can change, because everything is impermanent and it changes anyway, so by engaging with it through awareness you become able to influence the process. Meditation practice is fundamentally about sitting still, being open to your experience as it is, and meanwhile making an effort to focus on, say, the sensations of your breath (different meditation practices involve focusing on different things through progressive stages). What you quickly become aware of is two things; firstly it's incredible difficult to do, because in no time you find you've been thinking about something else, and secondly when you are able to concentrate, to focus, it is blissfully enjoyable. Once you experience that bliss you want more.

The snag is that you need to be able to focus in a wholehearted relaxed way, and this is very difficult if a part of you is jumping up and down saying, "Hey I'm a girl, I've gotta change to being more like a girl, like this!, and this!"

So I have had no choice in the end but to pursue a resolution of my transsexualism whilst at the same time deepening my practice of Buddhism. Going back to popular images of Buddhism in the movies it appears that all you have to do is to say you are a Buddhist, sip tea mindfully, and all your emotions have gone and you are calm as Dr Spock. It's actually more like sailing a fragile canoe down wild rapids; your raw experience is like the rapids, turbulent and with rocks in, and your new awareness, born of meditation, just manages to hold its own but can crumple on a rock at any minute. Meditating is a skill which you learn and the learning never stops because life never stops changing.

Whenever I meditated I was aware that my transsexualism was there, and I realised it caused me a lot of suffering.

Buddhism says that life involves suffering. I found this a relief because I realised that I was suffering, and that that wasn't my fault. I think our times can be difficult because we are supposed to enjoy life, and if we are not it's because we are not doing something right, we have a problem which needs fixing - by buying some new product, or a new dress, or a new therapy, or by ending this relationship and starting another.

Buddhism says that suffering inevitably follows all of these solutions because they are based on craving, and they are also impermanent. But the great thing is that impermanence also means there is a freedom for new things to grow; things can change, you do not have to be stuck with how you are. True change is not so much tinkering with your external life, it's more being able to change your attitudes - the really basic views that you have built up through your life which act as a filter, through which you see the world, which distort how you perceive things and other people affecting you, leading you to respond inappropriately, giving rise to yet more suffering, for others as well as yourself. It's a chain reaction thing, everybody's doing it. Buddhists see it as a wheel of misjudgements leading to inappropriate actions leading to further misjudgements, a constant movement of frustration and pain. But if you become more aware through practice, if you become interested in changing your deep-seated attitudes, then you cease to misjudge so much, you respond appropriately and you taste the wonderful taste of freedom.

Right from the beginning, I enjoyed learning about these ideas, which seemed to articulate what I had always felt, and I enjoyed exploring meditation.

What really attracted me was listening to talks on the theme of radical transformation, since I really disliked my current experience; the idea that I could change radically to become something else was exciting. Buddhism held out a promise that I could overcome suffering, including apparently my transsexualism, by achieving insight into the nature of Reality, by changing my `filter' so that I saw the world more how it really is.

This promise was very attractive because I didn't like being transsexual; it seemed to really mess your life up. What I had seen of other TSs didn't inspire me with confidence; they lost their families, their jobs, too many ended up depressed and on sickness benefit, they were often rather neurotic, and were resistant to the idea that anything about them could profitably be explored or changed.

This was where I was at for many years; I meditated daily, I attended my local Buddhist Centre where I found many friends, I went away on retreats at beautiful rural retreat centres for several weeks a year. I loved it; I felt I was going somewhere.

The problem was that after many years of practice I realised that the suffering emanating from my transsexualism was as strong as ever, it was like a turbulent rush of waters deep in my being. I could bury that experience temporarily, or I could sometimes transcend it in a rush of bliss as my meditation, suddenly released from the turbulence, soared into higher realms of consciousness, but in the end I had to get on with life, and that life included being transsexual. I tried all sorts of different strategies; tried just being it (how on earth do you do that?), I tried being open about it to my mystified friends, I tried writing the fantasies, or even some judicious acting out, which all helped a bit, but I kept coming back to the same point that whatever I did, the rushing turbulent waters were still there and my suffering led me to being grumpy and difficult, moody and preoccupied. And that meant that, as I saw it, there was a ceiling, a limit, on the effectiveness of my practice of meditation and on my ability to live an effective Buddhist life. However, up to this point I had earned the approval of my Buddhist seniors by, as we say, "Being aware of it and working on it." I was able to keep going because I still held out hope that somehow I could crack the thing through intense meditation practice.

What happened was the opposite; I did crack it, but by realising that although all things are impermanent, my transsexualism was part of my body (At this point I hear you all laughing and saying "Yea she finally got it!"). The hope I had of change 'through the inside' vanished, along with my motivation to continue to endure things as they were.

So having realised that my transsexual experience was there because it was part of my body, not a view or a belief or past Karma, and that it would pass when I died, but in the meantime would continue to give me hell, I thought that maybe I could reduce the suffering it caused by going to the doctor. So then began the next phase where I hoped to be able to manage things just by taking hormones, just to reduce the pain and suffering a bit, and meanwhile I'd carry on as normal.

Having already had the Charing Cross experience[1], I decided to go private, and went to see Russell Reid in London.

I feared that I had released the brake on a hugely powerful underground process and I feared the consequences for me and the life I had built up within the Buddhist movement – I had so much invested in my life as it was, and I was not confident that the Buddhist Order of which I am a part would be open to me transitioning from the men's part of the Order to the women's. (At least our Order was different from tradition in that there was ordination for women). The fear I felt was quite something; one bizarre effect, which took me quite a while to understand, was I started having stomach trouble; I kept burping. I would have episodes which would go on for hours, often half the day or more, which would only end when I went to bed. I tried diet changes, fasting, I went to the doctor, had tests at the hospital, it was really uncomfortable. It felt like my whole insides were full of air and no way could I get it out, I'd do these burps like a seal's bark, very embarrassing.

The doctor said I was swallowing air but I had no feeling of doing that, or that it was a response to fear. Eventually a friend said that maybe, when I felt wind in my stomach, I should concentrate simply on breathing evenly and let the sensation die away and it worked! What was happening was that the action of trying to release air from my stomach did the opposite and drew air down! It led me to practising being more mindful of the sensations in my stomach and that led me to becoming aware of the effects on me of coping, which I will come to later.

The hormones definitely helped for a couple of years but by then my appearance had begun to change and I was beginning to be taken for a woman in public – for example, when paying for some clothes with my debit card one day the cashier said, "This is your husband's card madam" (get out of that one!). It really is very weird never quite knowing how you are being perceived, and having to avoid public loos – thank goodness for the increasing number of unisex disabled loos! I finally cracked when I was in a big gathering of men Order members and just felt so deeply in the wrong place, and so many of them were beginning to respond to me in a funny way because they could see my increasingly womanly looks. I just phoned for a taxi and left. I couldn't cope with living the lie of being a man any more. The problem was that as far as others were concerned, they saw it the other way round; that my being a man was true, and my emerging femaleness was an artificially constructed lie.

I managed to give about 6 weeks' notice that I was going to transition which didn't go down very well in the wider Order, even locally with my friends. Because they saw me all the time, they couldn't see what I was making all the fuss about. I think they were fearful of me somehow being a shocking spectacle. There was a feeling amongst the more senior members of the women's wing of the Order that I had presented a fait accompli, that I had put myself in a difficult position and that the women's wing of the Order should feel no pressure to accept me. One of the senior men wrote to me saying he was baffled by my action and surely I was taking the conflict I felt within myself and projecting it out onto everyone else. I felt that these responses were a bit rich considering I had always been open about being transsexual and about how I was trying to work with it, and the situation I was in was partly a result of the culture in the Order and prevailing beliefs about gender. There is disbelief about the transsexual process. We are western Buddhists, and yet are we really open to the civilisation of which we are a part? A civilisation which has, through medical developments and social change, brought about the phenomenon of gender transition.

I mentioned above how inspiring I had found the talks about radical transformation, but I think that may lead to an exaggerated idea of the scope of change that can be brought about by meditation practice. When I look around me at my Buddhist friends, whom I have known for many years, I can see the effect that their practice has had, but it's radical in the sense that they have become kinder, wiser – they are still the same kind of person, recognisable, having the same character traits. If anything their uniqueness and individuality is more apparent, but nowhere do I see changes that are out of character, such as a non-numerate person becoming numerate, or a chronically untidy person becoming tidy. Those who had health problems back then still have them. The changes are qualitative, their quality of life is improved and they are more effective in their lives.

So you see my story of being a Buddhist and a Transsexual has moved through a number of episodes. My transition in the ordinary world was straightforward because I am very lucky to be small and I pass easily, and I had waited until the effects of the hormones proved that I was passing in public whilst making no real effort to do so (contrary to the Charing Cross model), but amongst the people I cared most about it has not been at all easy. The ideas and beliefs about gender held by my Buddhist friends meant they just did not believe me.

They believe that changing from a man to a woman is not possible. I have been as clear as I can that I have not changed from a 'man' to a 'woman' in the full sense of what is meant by being a man or a woman. I think that by being transsexual we are something different, we are in another place biologically; so for convenience I talk about myself as having been a transsexual living as a man, and I am now a transsexual living as a woman. There's no point me shouting out that I am a woman and have always been, which is what I feel, because why should they believe me? They don't believe in the whole business of gender identity contrary to external sex, and the consequences to a person of having Gender Dysphoria, which is the medical term for the condition I was battling with, because they have a simplified idea of what gender really is – 'a man is a man, and a woman is a woman'[2].

I've just mentioned the idea of consequences. One of the core insights of the Buddha was that actions have consequences, or rather, that your experience now is the consequence of an infinite network of previous actions by yourself and everything and everybody in the environment. So I have thought quite a bit about the consequences of being transsexual. Firstly there is the deep, deep underlying experience of uncertainty about what you are. It's like a sort of wobbling, you do not stand on firm ground, it wobbles. A common misunderstanding about Buddhism is that it involves going beyond the 'self'; actually it's more that you cannot find a 'self', no matter how hard you look, but we do need to have a healthy sense of ourselves in Order not to walk into things or walk all over others. I think being transsexual affects how our sense of self develops when we are children, because we have this wobbling, this uncertainty, which makes it very difficult to develop a healthy stable sense of self. It then follows that because our sense of self is unstable, uncertain, it's very difficult to develop healthy relationships with others. We mustn't get this out of proportion, because relatively few people develop a healthy sense of self anyway, but I put this forward because I'm trying to understand how I tick and most of my friends just don't seem to have to deal with an uncertain sense of self in this way. If you've grown up with this weird sense that you feel one thing about yourself inside, but the world around you keeps mirroring back the opposite, it has all sorts of consequences. I think it's hardly surprising many of us are a tad neurotic and obsessive. I think that what we discover is that the way to resolve uncertainty is to become certain, to be definite that you are the gender you feel yourself to be, regardless of what the world mirrors back to you. My Buddhist seniors wanted me to hang on in there with that uncertainty as my working ground. As my teacher said, "Why don't you work with your divided sense of yourself?" Well, it just leads to too much suffering, and I'd had enough.

Having transitioned, there then followed a lengthy consensus process within the women's side, or wing, of the Order, which went through several stages, over three years, where gradually I was accepted. I didn't enjoy being both the messenger for something and at the same time its ambassador. It wasn't very nice for me as I continued to be the focal point of others' uncertainty of me, but gradually it has evaporated.

You must be wondering why I didn't just do a runner and get out from amongst these people! I was very tempted, frequently, and was often despairing and bleak, and I still do get like that at times but I see it as an unavoidable part of my particular life experience which I need to ride out. The Order is really my family, my best friends are there, many of whom I have known for 20 years.

I feel a caution from my sisters in the Order, even now, around the role I can play in teaching women who are new to the movement. In most jobs one's gender is not important as long as you can do the job, but here everything is gender specific, and so gender is a core part, women teach women, because they have more in common, a common life experience even though they may have very different ethnic backgrounds.

My life experience has been so unusual; I have not had to work with the sort of issues that most women face when trying to commit to a Buddhist way of life. At the same time the issues I have had to work through, and what I have learned in the process, is so particular, so unusual as to not have much value, much currency. I may be wrong here but this is what I suspect.

However, I have been able to stay in the Order for which I am very glad.

Now, 7 years after going to the doctor and three years after surgery, the question is, have I been able to break through that ceiling I felt was there in my practice? Has it made the crucial difference?

From one point of view, the more physical and social, it has definitely worked. Testosterone did seem to do something horrible to me, and I felt instantly better without it. I am happy enough with my body as it is now; after surgery I felt an immediate improvement, although some aspects took some getting used to, like not having orgasms, and feeling so vulnerable. I was expecting to be quite sexually wild after surgery, but was unprepared for the intense feelings of physical vulnerability I felt during recovery and still do now. I'd need a very patient lover! How I am 'down there' is so utterly different to how I used to be, that it takes a while to get to know how it works, and part of that was waiting for everything to heal properly and get over the fear that all my insides were going to fall out if I sneezed. Also the surgery is so much more intricate and detailed than I thought was possible – it's like being given a gift. There's no comparison.

From the spiritual point of view I think transitioning and surgery has made my experience even more particular and individual – it's difficult to put into words, and difficult to share with my friends. The post-op experience is so, so different from the previous stages, it's like changing from being a powerboat with its engine on the wrong end to being a sailing dingy, it just doesn't compare. So I am practising with a very different living experience.

Part of this is to do with coping. I think we become very good at coping - being transsexual is so lonely, so unspeakable when we are young that we learn to cope with it. If you are coping with something unspeakable on a daily basis, you can get armoured, and other aspects of your experience disappear under the guarding layer too. Meditation practice meant I became aware of those coping mechanisms, but the op dissolved the final really big concrete block; what I called my Coping Stone, so now there isn't any part of my experience held back, buried, suppressed. But what has been revealed isn't very refined, so in meditation for much of the time I still experience a lot of turbulence but now it's more ordinary things like paranoia (nobody loves me!), anger and resentment and craving for a new kitchen. I don't feel the old gender angst anymore which is lovely.

One big fear I had was that I was giving in to craving, that my feeling that I was a woman, and my desire to be physically like a woman, was really just craving, a fantasy, and that when I had got it I would experience disappointment. This has not proved to be the case thankfully. It was the right thing to do. It would be good to be able to change my birth certificate; the continuing state of affairs in this country is a great cruelty and fuels people's doubts about the gender reassignment process.[3]

I think that having to face up to this experience, and stand-alone and face the loss of everything and come through it has made me more of a true being, a good Buddhist. And hopefully I still have many years left to me in this lifetime, as a (hopefully) wise old woman, to continue to deepen my practice.

[1] The Charing Cross approach is the care model used by the Charing Cross hospital, the main Gender Identity clinic in the UK, which insists that their patients transition and do a 'real life test' for a year before they will prescribe hormones. This consigns poorer people to living as a transvestite without the benefit of the physique changing effect of hormones. Many people resort to acquiring hormones on the internet to bypass these gatekeepers. Surgery is only available after the approved period of 'real life test' which involves proving you have been in a job – which may be an insuperable obstacle to many.

[2] I have now been able to change my birth certificate because the government, after years of lobbying from pressure groups, passed the appropriate laws to enable me to do that. I now have a new birth certificate. There is also an official method to enable me to do CRB checks whilst preserving my privacy. As a friend said – I was transsexual and have got better, it's not something I identify with, yet it's not a secret either. The support from this legal change has helped to soften the disbelief I had felt from my friends.

[3] See note 2 above.

# Joanne Cage / Modhuri: Not knowing

**The admission:** I want a safe and predictable universe.

**The solution:** Finding a glorious Truth that is permanent and creates a feeling of underlying joy.

**The problem:** Life is made up of certainty and uncertainty.

**The next step:** How do I live with not knowing?

**The dilemma:** One of the great declarations of the Kena Upanishad is 'If you think that you know, know that you know not,' and yet, paradoxically, the burning need to know makes us strive forward along the path. In the place of not knowing I have observed myself getting into difficult waters because it is incredibly painful not to know Instead of this being mysterious and exciting. I instead feel more like Arjuna at the start of his epic dialogue with Krishna – The Bhagavad Gita – sunken with grief and despair. The gaping silence at the end of a question is a space in which the mind feels like it is dying. I have been troubled, like many spiritual seekers, with often paralyzing questions such as, "How can I live fully when I know I am going to die?", "Is spirituality merely another distraction to make the unpredictable nature of life bearable, or does it point to a profound truth?", "Why has God placed me in a realm where I must inevitably lose everything I love?", "How can I act in life if all actions are meaningless in the face of eternity?", "Is God cruel and playing a sick joke?". I am speaking of questions that create states of mental agony so cavernous that it is difficult to be alive in these moments. As Manu Bazzano, a contemporary philosopher, succinctly puts it, "A sword hangs over us, held by a fine thread." It is an unnerving state of affairs! However the spiritual texts encourage us to stay in this empty space at the end of a question. For example, I take inspiration from Nachiketa in the Katha Upanishad. He stayed outside the house of Death for three days and nights waiting for Yama, Lord of Death, to answer his burning questions. In comparison I watch my mind scampering to find a solution after just three seconds let alone three days! Lost in a habitual rush to refill the unnerving gap created by not knowing, I have often neatly solidified a half-truth into an 'answer', just because it feels better.

However there are times when a question comes from deep within and then it has its own incredible momentum. Ramesh Balsekar says that we do not ask the question, the question arises. In these moments, answers cooked up by the mind feel like a sticking plaster over a mile deep wound. Here the mind is suddenly aware that it is trying to bridge the universe with a matchstick and it humbly stops its game, red-faced and exhausted. I now recognise this state as fertile ground for insight because there is something about complete uncertainty that alters the normal functioning of the mind. Swami Nishchalananda says that meditation is about creating space in order that insight can arise. It is only insight that can help heal these wounds. Otherwise the mind goes around and around and the answers to life's deeper questions simply do not arise at the level of the thinking mind.

**The Insight:** It was a glorious moment when I realised that angst and confusion is a perfectly valid response to this rather peculiar existence. I resonate with Rumi when he says, "Sell your cleverness and buy bewilderment." After a particularly excruciating few hours of mental turmoil the insight arose that I am not meant to know the answer to some of life's questions. Somehow it removed a weight from my heart. I could stop striving for the impossible. I could trust rather than know. From a deep place I accepted that this universe is a mystery and that was simply and beautifully OK. Life no longer feels like an unsolvable puzzle that I am hopelessly compelled to keep trying to crack. This allows me to see that anxiety and bewilderment are not unhealthy mental states from which I need to liberate myself, but can be gateways to insight. Indeed emotions that are too lukewarm; "Never threaten to undo the self; they safeguard it in a limbo where loss is never fully experienced, and thus never resolved." Therefore pain is no longer a sign of failure in my spiritual practice but as miraculous and as necessary as love. Why is this? I don't know! But I feel that each time I get acclimatised to the sickly altitude of not knowing, my heart softens, I embrace more and, most importantly, my sense of awe and love for God increases.

Swami Nishchalananda says that without ignorance we would not exist as embodied beings. Accepting ignorance as an essential part of this life is an incredibly tender and liberating perspective to have towards ourselves and others. Bazzano also celebrates ignorance when he states that we find ourselves in a universe "where nature has thrown away the key, where the code is unknown, and we have no other task but to delight in reality's ambiguity." No other task but to delight. Swami Nishchalananda teaches a profound practice from the Vijnana Bhaivara Tantra in which we are asked to reflect on everything as a revelation of Reality. It is extraordinary to catch a glimpse of both sadness and joy revealing Reality in equal measure.

**Conclusion:** The spiritual path is a curious mix of knowing, at times with such wonder and at other times being immersed in the pain of not knowing. I have moved from fighting against not knowing to a prayer that I may always be bewildered, and that I may always celebrate the unfathomable mystery of God. I experienced tumbling into the void of my own eventual nothingness and then, by God's grace, a fire in my belly that told me I was going to live anyway! Mary Oliver expresses this exquisitely when she states "clearly I am not needed yet I feel myself turning to something of inexplicable value. It is a daily adventure to live with this dual realisation. Ignorance and insight are deeply interlaced strands in the tapestry of life. Tennessee Williams, the American playwright, stated that life is an unanswerable question, but added a word of encouragement: that we should also 'believe in the dignity and importance of the question'." Amen to that.

*Joanne / Modhuri had a Christian upbringing in Suffolk. She is now a member of the community of a Hindu Ashram in Wales where she teaches yoga.*

# John Peck:

# Autobiography of a retired Baptist Minister

I am interested in football. I like watching games on TV, studying the different strategies of different teams and players, and sometimes cheering when the weaker team scores a goal. I'm not a fan; the price of tickets is way too high. And, apart from kicking a ball about with my children, I haven't played. This may a strange introduction to a life-story of faith, but surely there many people for whom football functions as a religion, and my attitude to it almost exactly parallels my religious attitude for the first 18 years of my life.

I have only three memories of any involvement with religion during that time. One was sitting in a Sunday School class, listening to the teacher. What she said went right past me; no wisp of memory remains. Another was once when instead of Sunday school, I had spent the collection on a comic, and was reading it in our tube station when my father came to catch his train, and I hid in terror. The third was when I had been caught stealing a book from the primary school library, and I was standing under judgement before Miss Hillcox the headmistress, who, in the course of her serious rebuke said, "And you know, don't you, who you ought to be following and trying to copy?", and of course I missed the correct answer; "Jesus."

During the whole time, stealing was my strong point; from the school, from fellow pupils, from shops, and anyone within reach. Almost all the time I got away with it, even while I was at Haberdashers' Aske's public school, which was where along with the rest of the class I went through confirmation, somewhat rebelliously, for I recall deliberately chewing gum through the whole ceremony. But then, during the last year of school, God caught up with me.

There were four of us in the 'scholarship class,' and we used to spend a lot of our time discussing all the teenage preoccupations, religion among them. One of the four was an odd character who always talked about God like He was his next-door neighbour. I prided myself on being open-minded, so I listened with polite seriousness. It grew on me, and gradually I began to feel, vaguely, that it had to be taken seriously.

One day, as the two of us were cycling to the public library, Alan asked me point-blank, "Are you a Christian?" Well I'd been to church, my parents had got me to say my prayers, and I was interested in religion including other religions. But much to my own surprise I found myself saying "No". So Alan started talking… We cycled around for a long time. Then he said, "John, do you believe that Jesus Christ died to save you from your sins?" Well, I'd been taught all that sort of thing, so, quite casually, I said "… er, Yes." He said, "Then you're a Christian!"

To this day, I have no idea what happened to my thinking at that point. All I do know is that when I got home, I went to my bedroom, knelt by the bed, and said a prayer. And I knew, beyond a shadow of doubt, that I was being heard. Life has never been the same since.

Alan told me more, in particular that I must not hide my faith, so I talked to my closest school friend about it, and he cut me dead. When I was fire watching (it was wartime, 1942) I knelt to say my prayers, and could hear the others whispering together… Time went by; I realised I'd got to do something about the stealing, so I started giving things back where I could. I remember sending some money to Marks and Spencer's with a confessing letter. The reply was fascinating; clearly the recipients were completely bewildered and at a loss!

Since then, that initial prayer led me into a life of ongoing dialogue with God; I learned to recognise His way of speaking directly into my thoughts in a way which forced me into honesty, clarified my confusions, challenged in ways that often appeared utterly unpredictable, yet turned out to make enormous sense.

The next 66 years were packed with eventful experience –

Travel, visiting Italy, Switzerland, France, Germany, Spain, Greece, Balkans, Egypt, Turkey, Holy Land, India & Nepal.

War-service as a 'conscie' on a farm.

Preaching as a lay reader, Christian Endeavour, Methodist local preacher.

Bible College training, where I learned Hebrew.

Village evangelism with a faith mission.

Screen-printing in Birmingham.

Married life, fostering.

Becoming a Baptist minister.

Lecturing at Bible Training College.

Involvement with Greenbelt Arts Festival.

Writing and school teaching.

Lecturing in Ipswich, Colchester, Cambridge, Holland, Switzerland, and USA.

I have been led through stages of thought and behaviour I never imagined.

The six years with faith mission taught me to live intelligently with miracles.

- There was a time of crisis when I found myself allowing God's Spirit to take over my life, and give it power to bless people.
- During my early travels, encounters with people of other cultures and religions enlarged my understanding of my own faith, especially when a time came for me to see the Bible in a new light, not merely as a religious book, but as the literature of a people whose world-view had been formed by the God and Father of Jesus Christ.
- That took me into the founding and growth of Greenbelt, with its vision of a distinctively Christian understanding of art and the secular world, which then led to a few years of 'College House', an institution which I founded for teaching.

Some other experiences specially stand out, for which I am profoundly grateful.

- My mother's teaching – I was learning French songs before primary age;

- My father's skills in discussion, which taught me to see both sides of an argument, and could talk with me till I confessed to lying – so my primary experience of God was of One who would see through any attempt at dishonesty or pretence.
- My mother's need for a travel escort which put me in direct contact with people and cultures of so many different religions, and to learn so much from them.
- The way farming gave me space to learn how to live as a Christian, and to experience the fullness of the Holy Spirit.
- My parents' willingness to pay for my training, and the faith mission which taught me how to live with miracles. Over the years, the kindness and generosity of so many people through whom those miracles were wrought.
- The gift of a wife for forty years whose insight, courage, endurance, love, was unostentatiously gigantic, especially in caring for so many foster-children as well as our own family.
- The privilege of involvement in the ideology of Greenbelt, enabling me to put into practice insights into my faith which it had taken me about thirty years to discover and understand!
- The discovery of an openheartedness and generosity about American people which I had never known from the media.
- The pleasure of converse with people of other faiths through SIFRE which so often casts fresh light on my own.

In all that, God has preserved me from doing many silly things, and shielded me from suffering as much as others whom I have known. He has often spoken and guided me in ways that bewildered, even frightened me, but which turned out to be so obviously right, sometimes done with what must have demonstrated His sense of humour! The last years have made me vividly aware of God as Love on a cosmic scale, which Jesus redefined for us in terms of His service, and I am still learning… not for nothing does Scripture call Christians disciples!

# Joy van Helvert:

# At home within Nichiren Buddhism

I first met this practice 25 years ago, just after my first child was born. Running up to her birth the burgeoning responsibility of parenthood seemed to add urgency to my search for answers to questions about the purpose of being alive. Senses honed to all things spiritual, I started to read about different faiths and practices and to open my life to some new ideas. It soon became apparent that Buddhism was my natural spiritual home; a deep respect for the dignity and sanctity of life, the cyclical nature of birth and death, and the notion that we ourselves are the divine "stuff" of the universe in contrast to being in a relationship with an external and omnipotent being, all seemed to resonate with me at the deepest level. I read some of the classic Buddhist texts then finally decided to visit a retreat centre in Hemel Hempstead; it was a truly wonderful experience. However, back in daily life the practice was difficult to sustain. Enlightenment appeared to be a lofty ideal far removed from the realities of paying the bills, earning a living and bringing up children. I was faced with a dilemma; on the one hand I felt the urge to detach myself from the maelstrom of the 9 to 5, the tensions of family life and the general social milieu, on the other hand, I had a good job that I enjoyed doing, a loving family I wanted to be part of, and many close friendships worth preserving. So I put the journey on hold.

When my daughter was a few months old I came across some literature produced by the lay organisation **Soka Gakkai International** (SGI) about Nichiren Buddhism. At first I was intrigued by the pictures of very ordinary relaxed smiling people that seemed somehow to be lit from the inside. The ever-present cynic in me wondered how they'd managed to orchestrate such natural looking images. There were no monks, nuns, robes or sandals, people seemed to be from a very diverse range of ethnic backgrounds, and a wide range of ages.

I made some enquiries and eventually decided to attend a local discussion meeting. So with no idea what to expect and a certain amount of trepidation, I found myself knocking on the front door of a small semi-detached house in Braintree one evening. After a warm welcome I was ushered into the living room where six or seven people were chanting "Nam-Myoho-Renge-Kyo" in front of a scroll with odd-looking characters on it that was hung inside a small cupboard, not much bigger than a box of A4 paper. It seemed strange but also somehow familiar and uplifting. The chanting was followed by a discussion based on Buddhist principles in which people talked about their personal experiences of practicing of Nichiren Buddhism. I was moved by their openness and honesty and inspired by the way they faced and overcame the issues they encountered in daily life.

By the end of the evening I'd come to understand that Nam-Myoho-Renge-Kyo is the name of a natural principle or law governing the workings of life in the universe and that chanting is an expression of our personal determination to live and act in harmony with this law. When I asked why there were no statues of the Buddha, I was told that rather than chanting or meditating in front of an image representing the life of the historical Buddha (Shakyamuni), Nichiren had instead directed his followers to focus on a scroll called the Gohonzon (honourable object of worship) which represents the Buddha qualities (wisdom, courage, compassion and life energy – our greater self) existing in our own lives and in the lives of all others without exception. The Gohonzon, then, is a kind of mirror, and chanting to it helps us reflect on and develop our own lives and our concern and compassion for others in society. Thus, from the perspective of Nichiren Buddhism, Buddhahood is a dynamic state we can choose to manifest and cultivate; it's not something beyond the reach of ordinary people in their current lifetime.

Over the years, this profound and pragmatic practice has become part of my daily life. Its values and philosophy have been the tree under which my husband and I have brought up four children, two of whom have chosen to practice themselves. It has given me a sense of purpose and enriched my life by taking me down paths and connecting me to people and experiences I could never have imagined. It has changed the way I look at the world, how I feel about myself and what I see in others. Of course, life is sometimes difficult and the inner cynic still exists but for the most part it occupies a much less dominant role - I gossip less, slander less, face my problems and sleep better at night!

Small, friendly discussion meetings, like the one I attended in Braintree twenty-five years ago, happen in cities, towns and villages all over the country on a monthly basis. For more information see **www.sgi-uk.org**.

# Khatereh Vahdat:

# Born in Iran; living in Suffolk

Allah'u'Abha (an Arabic phrase meaning "God the All-Glorious"), is the word Bahá'ís use to greet each other. So I would like to say to all of you, Allah'u'Abha.

My life in Suffolk started in 1994, immediately after my graduations from Middlesex University in London, obtaining a Master of Engineering in Microelectronics Design and Production. This, I say, is rather interesting to me at least. My background routes back to my birth place Iran, where I was expelled from Sommayeh school in Shiraz for my belief in the Bahá'í Faith!

After graduating, I left London as I found a contract job as a research associate with BT Laboratories, where we worked on the first high speed Internet access to homes (in technical terms it was called ADSL), and after few months in February 1995, I was employed full time there.

In my spare times, I spent the next few years in promoting faith in the society. In Felixstowe, I had many Bahá'í youth activities to promote the principles of the Bahá'í Faith; One God, One Faith and One Mankind. I then moved to Ipswich and extended the activities to Ipswich, Lowestoft and Cambridge and became an active member of the Local Assembly in Ipswich, supporting the annual Mayor's interfaith service and many other activities promoting peace and love.

In the late 1990s, I started to travel with my BT work to Europe. Now as a consultant, I had a lot to offer. It was interesting to me that in every city I entered I had a family there, the Bahá'í community. They invited me to their homes and sometimes I participated in their peace promoting activities too. In the winter of 1999, I chose to stay in Rome for my work. The beauty of that city captured my eyes and I pitched my tent in central Rome near Piazza Spanga (the Spanish Steps), where I also contributed to the Bahá'í activities to promote love and unity. I held gatherings in my home and the subject of our activities were mainly 'Amore' of the soul. I visited the orphanage at the top of the nearby Piazza Popolare, which was run by the church there. A few times I visited the orphan children and took gifts and toys. They were so happy to receive them and we sung Christian songs together. I also met my husband in Rome – for romance!

In the spring of 2001, I was happy to return to my home in Ipswich, when I fell pregnant with my twin boys. I left my work as I concentrated in bringing up my children. Now I have 4 children and live in Ipswich. This year in September, I decided to study for a part time PGCE and have started to work as a supply teacher in the schools. I am a member of the Bahá'í Local Assembly in Ipswich. I am also an active participant in the great church services of St Margaret's Church, which is well placed centrally in a beautiful area of Ipswich adjacent to Christchurch Park. Three of my children sing in the church choir and I would like to invite you all to come and join the church service on Sunday mornings to see them singing!

I often think of two key words, "faith" and "hate", and how they are sometimes confused. Bahá'u'lláh has taught me to look at the light and not at the lamp. By practising that, I have learnt to love Christ as much as I love Bahá'u'lláh, Mohammed, Buddha and …

Over the years I have been the subject of unnecessary hatred as well as abounding love by the people of faith. I feel that our advanced civilization is threatened and hanging over these two simple words. The result of one is spiritual attainment and glorification in all realms of life and the outcome of the other is chaos and confusion, war and famine and destruction of our well-established societies. Let's be of the people of faith. This is the key to our future holdings.

# Margaret Nelson: The problem with labels

The older I get, the less I'm inclined to adopt any label to describe how I view life, the universe, and everything. The trouble with labels is that they encourage laziness. If you're in a social situation and someone asks you what you do, or what you are, and you tell them, they'll be inclined to refer to whatever they've heard or read about that label and apply it to you. It's more interesting to be mysterious; to learn about each other through a process of discovery. Labels lead to pre-conceived ideas about what they stand for. If someone identifies him or herself as a Christian or a Muslim, what do you assume about him or her, and his or her attitudes to, say, morality or privilege? You're likely to be wrong. We form our values and opinions through our experience and the people and ideas that have influenced us, including religious ideas, and we react to these things differently.

So, if I describe myself as a Humanist, some may assume that I'm part of a trend towards what a friend calls "fluffy, cuddly Humanism", which can be summarised as simply being good without God. In its campaign for legal humanist weddings in England and Wales, the British Humanist Association has, perhaps unintentionally, given the impression that everyone who has a Humanist rite of passage celebration (a Humanist ceremony) is a Humanist, and that Humanism is equivalent to religion, which it isn't.

Humanism, to me, is a way of thinking, of viewing the world, in the only way we can; as human beings, without reference to any supernatural explanations for life, the universe, and everything. The philosopher Bertrand Russell said, "Many people would sooner die than think. In fact they do." I'm not sure that he was entirely right, as it seems to me that not thinking isn't necessarily a choice; some people are just not very curious. A Humanist friend was asked, "Don't you have to be really brainy to be a Humanist?" "No," she replied, "you just have to use the brains you've got." Humanism is a philosophy for the insatiably curious, who never stop asking questions. Far from being fluffy and cuddly, humanism can sometimes lead you to lonely places, but it can also be bracing to find yourself in a different place from other people, discovering things for yourself. Humanists habitually ask "Why?" Sometimes, there isn't an answer.

This approach to life has been described as a scientific one; science is defined as the systematic study of the structure and behaviour of the physical and natural world through observation and experiment. It's also been claimed as a philosophical approach, since philosophy is the study of the fundamental nature of knowledge, reality, and existence. But we're back to labels again, and possibly the claims of different disciplines, when a Humanist approach to life is limitless. Creative expression through the arts, social innovation, psychology, political theory, the evolving uses of language, are all avenues through which we're free to explore, if we choose.

How did I get here? As a child, I drove my parents and teachers mad by constantly questioning what I was told. My parents, whose families originated in Scotland, were raised as Presbyterians – a rather dour bunch of non-conformists who disapproved of the pleasures of the senses, particularly on Sundays. Mum, who enjoyed a wee dram, didn't appear to be wholly convinced by this brand of Christianity and, like many others, developed her own, private version, which didn't involve going to church. Dad did go to church until his deafness meant he couldn't follow the services. I was sent to church, and the church youth club, where I got into trouble for arguing with the minister. By the time I was in my early teens, having explored some alternative ways of thinking in the public library and with a friend's more liberal parents, I announced I didn't believe any of it, and that was that. I wasn't put under any pressure to continue going to church. A Quaker RE teacher listened to some of my half-formed ideas and didn't try to impose any kind of orthodoxy, which helped. By the time I left school at sixteen to work in a bank, religion played no part in my life. It has been an irrelevance ever since.

Going to Art College and university in the 1960s and early 1970s brought me into contact with bright people from a wide range of disciplines, as well as some students whose upbringing had been far more religious than mine. One sad case was a boy who'd been raised a Catholic and who found it hard to cope with all the students' sexual activity going on around him. Deeply conflicted, he had a breakdown and was found wandering the streets naked late one night. Another Catholic friend coped by spending a lot of time in the confessional, joking that they'd had to install a loo in there, just for him. At university, studying for a post-graduate teaching qualification with an assortment of graduates from all disciplines, one of my tutors was the mathematician Dick Tahta, who'd inspired Stephen Hawking as a schoolboy. Dick was very keen on existentialism. He took a small group of us for an intense weekend in a remote bungalow owned by the Monkton Wyld Centre in Dorset. To this day, I'm still not sure what the purpose of this weekend was, and I'm none the wiser about existentialism (a rather nihilistic movement), but Dick encouraged us to question just about everything, which some of us did. One friend, a fellow artist, took to spending a lot of time in the garden playing his violin. If I could remember more about it, it would make a good film. Dick was among several of the staff at college and university who encouraged a non-conformist approach to life and although I didn't end up with particularly impressive qualifications, as I was never very good at sticking to a syllabus, I'm forever grateful to them.

It wasn't until much later, over twenty years later, that I got involved with organised Humanism. At that time, the British Humanist Association was a small organisation that campaigned against religious privilege and encouraged non-religious people to openly reject the status quo, where the church claimed the moral high ground and dominated public ceremonial, and children were not taught about alternatives to Christianity, including the freethinking alternative. I had surgery and treatment for cancer and soon afterwards my parents died within six months of one another. These events led me to consider what sort of funeral my son might arrange for me, as it wouldn't be appropriate to invite God. Funeral directors only offered religious funerals, so I volunteered to become a humanist celebrant in 1991. In December that year, I founded the Suffolk Humanist group, where like-minded people have met to share ideas and raise awareness of alternatives to religion. The rest, as they say, is history. After those first few years, most people became aware that religious ministers don't have a monopoly of rite of passage ceremonies, which can be as personal as you choose. What started as a small subversive movement has resulted in a widespread rejection of convention. Humanists still have a role to play, but we're among many who offer a choice. What most people don't realise is that we were here first.

Having given over twenty years as a secular subversive, I'm no longer very active in organised Humanism but I'll be a freethinker until the day I die, unless I go doolally, in which case, I won't care.

# Mayuri Patel: My Hindu story

I live in South Ipswich with my two teenage daughters aged 17 and 14, and my husband Chandresh. We have a small family retail business and I also work as an accounts assistant at Ipswich and Suffolk Council for Racial Equality.

I was born in the Gujarat state of India and grew up in an extended family in Bombay surrounded by uncles, aunties, cousins and of course my parents and my lovely little sister! We used to have a small shrine in our house and worshipped several different deities, including Krishna, Ganesh, Saraswati, Laxmi and Swaminarayan. We also went to our Mandir regularly to celebrate birthdays, wedding anniversaries, Diwali, and just before our exams and after our results to say thanks to God. We used to go to our native village every summer in the holidays to see our grandparents.

At school we also celebrated Hindu holidays like Diwali, Holi, Makar Sankrati and many other religious festivals. Every day at school our typical day would start with prayers before lessons. During the Diwali time we used to bring sweets to the school and shared them with each other. We had rangoli competitions, lantern making, and occasionally we decorated our notebooks as it was the start of the New Year. At my college The Gita (the holy book) was a subject that we had to study, in many schools it was a compulsory subject! I loved learning about all of our Hindu pasts and all of our 'psalms', as you could call them.

After marriage I joined my husband in Ipswich in 1994. At that time, there were very few Hindu families in Ipswich and no place to worship, which meant that there were not enough of us to form a community so that we could properly celebrate our festivals. For example, the Navrati festival had to be celebrated at the house of one of our friends. It was enjoyable but it did not measure up to the way that we used to celebrate back home! However, during those times we got by, by worshipping in our shrine and often visiting the Neasden temple in London to celebrate and thank God for anniversaries, birthdays and religious festivals that have gone by. Before we worship in the shrine, we bathe and clean ourselves, next we pray to God for future success and happiness and finally we use prayer beads and thank God for everything that we have been given.

As the years passed, more and more Hindu families arrived in Ipswich. We all felt that there should be a place in Ipswich where we could all get together and properly celebrate our festivals. This was how the Ipswich Hindu Samaj was formed; this was also when the idea came up of establishing a Mandir in Ipswich. Today, this is the place where we go to pray, get together for functions and set up various clubs for the elderly and the young. For example, each Wednesday lunchtime there is an elderly luncheon club. I think that this is a really important part of our Indian culture- we always look after and respect our elderly.

Hinduism is all about learning, and most of what my children have learned, they have learned by observing their elders and absorbing their values – respect and honesty in particular. But there is probably another reason they respect elders; because they strictly believe in Karma and don't want to be reincarnated into something small.

The Hindu community is growing, however, I feel that many children are often at a loss and do not have many opportunities to fully embrace the religion. To overcome this problem, I feel that we should try and encourage the children to participate in the events linked to our religion, to ensure that they fully understand it and appreciate our culture. My daughters like the idea of being Hindu, though mostly they love the culture side of it – they love the colours and music involved with the many different festivals! My main aim is to ensure that my daughters will carry on and continue the Hindu religion and culture into their families.

# Nayan Shah: Who am I?

*Nayan came to Suffolk to study*

My name meaning eyes.
My roots background — Father House of Mewor
Mother House of Travencore
Father Aryan, Digamber Jain
Mother Dravidian, Jacobite Syrian Orthodox Christian
Both Indian origin so am I and the religion of the family
(that includes me) are both.
By root I am Aryan.
Religion is not questioned but accepted. No question has an answer
it can have many or no answers.
I was born into two religions and thus I follow both.
I am currently a SIFRE tutor for both faiths
and a student at UCS in BSc (Hons) S.E.
My future ambition is to study a masters in S.E. or Internet Studies
Working for SIFRE gives the feeling of being a valued member
of the local community.
If I do leave Ipswich (because my course is not offered here)
then I would like to carry on the same kind of work in other "IFREs".
My name means eyes,
My favourite sport is swimming,
I am a whiz with computers tho' not a geek!
I like to eat pizzas and no, I am not one.
But I am an excellent disaster in the kitchen.
TV is my addiction, so is sleeping – that's only when I am at home
At college I study hard, work hard,
and thus get a chance to relax when at home.
My career is my ambition,
I guess that makes me a career-minded person.
What else can I say, get to know me and I will say
Who am I?

# Patric Standford: The birth of an Oratorio

It all began in 1969 as a short piece of music I wrote for a remarkable choral conductor called John Alldis, who exerted a demanding technique on his choir, the unwritten motto of which (he told me) was, "The difficult we sight-read; the impossible takes a couple of rehearsals." The piece was a setting of *Stabat Mater,* the prayer offered by the Mother of Christ at the foot of the cross as she held vigil during His last few hours. For me it became a musical devotion that I felt could be dedicated to anyone enduring the final hours of life on earth.

I had at that time been a professor of musical composition at the Guildhall School of Music & Drama in London for only a couple of years. The principal of the School, Allen Percival, heard the piece, and asked me if it would be possible for me to expand it, making of it a large-scale Easter Oratorio into which the entire resources of the School could be concentrated. This not only meant a large choir, a specialist 'chamber choir', all the School's orchestral players and brass band, but also a team of students from the drama and dance department – as well as the thirty-odd treble voices of the junior music school choir.

And so it became my *Christus-Requiem,* a huge two-hour Easter performance that filled St Paul's Cathedral for an evening in March 1973. In the crowded audience were the Chief Rabbi and the acting head of the Russian Orthodox Church, monks from Ealing Abbey alongside a contingent of Chinese Buddhists, and perhaps representatives of other religions, for the school had a large mixed body of oriental students.

I decided to devote the first half to a dramatic representation of the crucifixion in which I could mix German Protestant chorales with Catholic Latin hymns, quotations from the Christian Gospels, the Apocrypha and Thomas à Kempis, as well as Hebrew and Aramaic texts. The second half would be a meditation in many tongues, using poems in French, German, Russian, Italian, Latin and Czech (I had to stop somewhere!).

There were a few challenges. The most pressing was a representation by members of the student's Christian Union who, having attended the first full rehearsal, said they did not wish to be a part of Pilate's crowd that called for Christ's crucifixion. A small group did not wish to take part in a performance in a Cathedral. When I came to proofread the programme, it was apparent that Psalm 22, for which I used the original Hebrew, was printed upside-down!

The good offices of the school's staff and the City of London Fathers, whose support was invaluable to the enterprise, worked gentle magic to resolve these and several other complications, both inter-faith and musical, amicably. The performance was a huge success for the City of London and its famous School.

*Sadly Patric died on 23 April 2014, aged 75. Having had a highly successful career as a diverse composer and teacher, he had recently retired to Suffolk. His demeanour was modest, but his achievements were remarkable. His Christus Requiem (see above) drew on texts in seven languages.*

# Prabjot Kaur:

## Taking Amrit: my initiation ceremony

I had wished to take Amrit from a long time. I used to see my older sister and nieces who were Amritdahari (a person who has taken Amrit) who wore a kheski (a small form of a turban.) When I visited them their way of life was different from ours. They would wake up in the early hours of the morning and be reciting prayers. Although, at home we would always do morning prayers before starting our daily routine, to me it seemed they had more a peaceful way of life. At that time we had a grocery store which was very long hours for 7 days a week. The store was run by my husband, children and me, and it was very hard work. For this reason, my time was taken up mostly with raising a family and running the store, leaving little time for spirituality.

I was raised in Manchester and recall that in the 1960s, my parents read prayers morning and evening and also played Kirtan (melodic Sikh hymns) on the big spool tapes. We went to the Gurdwara (place of worship) regularly with our parents. The love for gurbani (sayings of the Gurus) and Kirtan (spiritual chanting) started from there. My gran was a devoted religious person and when I was about 8 or 9, lying in bed, I used to listen to her reciting prayers when we went and stayed in our school holidays. Although at the time I didn't understand the prayers, later when I grew older I recognised them and this early introduction to prayers helped guide me in taking the path towards spirituality. My gran also used to tell us stories about the Gurus.

I got married in 1964 and came to Ipswich. At the time, I couldn't understand why Ipswich didn't have a Gurdwara. My father in law would make prasad (made from semolina, butter, and sugar) and recite prayers at home on a Sunday. There was not a large Sikh Community in Ipswich at that time.

Years later, the Sikh families of Ipswich got funds together and bought a house which they made into a Gurdwara. I used to go to Manchester or London if I wanted to go to an all-night Kirtan called Raensbai, where one would see a lot of sangat (spiritual communities) and when they would recite VaheGuru (God's name), it appeared that they couldn't stop and it was like they were in a trance. My yearning to take Amrit and follow a spiritual path grew as the years went by. Years later in 1994, we closed our shop and some of our children had got married and moved away and life was less busy. However, years had gone passed and I was growing older.

In 1998, my daughter-in-law had gone to visit her parents in Southall when she phoned to say they are doing an Amrit Sanchar programme (baptism ceremony), on Sunday at the Gurdwara. She said that she wanted to take Amrit and wanted my son to take it as well.

I felt like this was my chance finally to take Amrit. I asked my husband if he wanted to take it as well but he said he was not ready for it yet. I went with my son and daughter-in-law and stayed round her parents' house. We were really excited and got up at 2.30 am, bathed, and went to the Gurdwara by 3 am. There was a Shri Akhand Paath Sahib, which involved the Guru Granth Sahib being read by Granthis (learned people who are able to read the Guru Granth Sahib), from start to finish without stopping and it takes approximately 48 hours. After the recital had finished, there was Kirtan. Then we were called to a room and before we entered a Bhai Sahib (a spiritual Sikh person) stopped me and asked where my husband was. I explained that he said that he was not ready to take Amrit yet. He said we like to give Amrit to couples only so that they lead the same way of life together as an Amritdahari (Baptised Sikh) couple. I was so disappointed but who was I to oppose the Spiritual one's decision so I did not take Amrit that day. However, my son and his wife then took Amrit.

I can understand now why it was said that a couple should take Amrit together. I left eating meat and became a vegetarian from that day, and waited for my turn as I was still very determined. It had changed my way of life as I tried to get up early and recited the prayers. The following year was 1999 and in April it was a very special year for our Sikhs as it was going to be 300 years to the Birth of the Khalsa which happened in 1699. In January that year I heard on the radio that they were doing Amrit Sanchar (Sikh initiation ceremony) at Southall Gurdwara. I decided this was my chance. I told my family and two of my sons with their wives wished to go with me. It had been snowing the night before and was a very cold day but I got up early and bathed and washed my hair and wore my new Khachera (undergarment, one of the 5 Ks).

We started our journey to Southall. I was so excited thinking, is it really happening? We arrived at the Gurdwara and a couple of hours later, we went to the Deewan Hall (main prayer hall), paid respects to the Guru Granth Sahib Ji and received prasad. The Bhai Sahib announced that those members of the Sangat that wished to take Amrit should take the five Ks, which were Kara (steel bracelet), Khanga (comb), Khecheraa (undergarment), and Kirpan (plus uncut hair), if they needed them before taking Amrit. Some of the sangat had already received a kirpan and ghatharaa (a holder for the kirpan) as well as a khanga. I bowed down to the Guru Granth Sahib ji and asked God, "VaheGuru, please bless me with your precious gift of Amrit". We went back upstairs in a special room where the Sangat were receiving Amrit. This time, there were a lot of ladies alone and men as well. The Bhai Shib didn't say anything. We were taken into a white painted room where in the middle was the holy book, Guru Granth Sahib Jee, and were told to pay respects and sit down. The atmosphere was so amazing and peaceful. The Panj Pyara (5 baptised Sikhs) came in and dressed in their robes of orange and royal blue, and carrying large kirpans. They brought the large steel bowl filled with water and into the bowl they put pattasea (a type of Punjabi sugar cube).

We sat and watched the Panj Pyara recite prayers. Each prayer, Japji sahib, Jaap sahib, Tav Prasad Savaiye, Chaupai Sahib, and Anand

Sahib – it took over an hour to recite them. Then we were told by a Bhai Sahib to go to one of the Panj Pyaraa. When it was my turn, they gave Amrit in my hands, five times to drink and say to VaheGuru, "Ji-khalsa VaheGuru ji ki Fateh" (The Khalsa belongs to the Lord and victory belongs to the Lord also). I drank the Amrit and then a Panj Pyara poured Amrit five times on my head and five times into my eyes. It was sugary water, so quite tasty. I recited "VaheGuru ji ka Khalsa, VaheGuru ji ki Fateh" each time.

Once everyone had finished taking the Amrit, they then explained to us about the Sikh code of conduct and what you should and shouldn't do as an Amritdahari Sikh. We were told to wake up in the early hours of the morning and recite the five prayers that the Panj Pyaraa had recited which were Japji Sahib, Jaap Shib, Tav Prasad Savaiye, Chaupai Sahib, and Anand Sahib. In addition, Reharas Sahib was to be recited in the evening and Kirtan sohila was recited before going to sleep. You were also told to repeat VaheGuru as many times as you can in the day.

It has been 14 years since I took Amrit and it has been a wonderful journey. I am still learning as a Sikh. In fact, Sikh means learner and I learn something about my faith every day. I still love listening to Kirtan and reciting prayers with Guru jee's blessings.

# Punna Athwall:

# The Sikh way of life: A personal perspective

This essay presents an overview of the Sikh way of life and how the author's life experiences in the Punjab and England have influenced his understanding of religious life. This material is used to address the issue of personal identity and why the author has not been able to fully embrace the Sikh way of life.

Guru Nanak was the founder of the Sikh religion and he had his first mystic experience in 1499 at the age of thirty-nine years (Singh, 2004, pp 31). The core message of Guru Nanak was to go into the world to pray and teach mankind how to pray and that it was important to let one's life embrace the praise of the Word, charity, ablution, service and prayer. Guru Nanak travelled extensively throughout India and as far as Baghdad. On his travels he was accompanied by a Muslim minstrel, Mardana. During the next 200 years, the nine Gurus who followed Guru Nanak helped to establish the Sikh community. This included the composition of the Sikh holy book, the Granth Sahib, and the building of the Golden Temple as the main Sikh shrine.

During this period the Punjab was ruled by the Mughals and Emperor Aurangzeb had started converting Hindus and Sikhs to Islam by force. They had no one to defend them! On the occasion of the first day of Vaisakhi in 1699, the tenth Guru decided to raise a new community to be called the Khalsa. He baptised five men in a new manner. The five who had until then belonged to different castes were made to drink out of one bowl to signify their initiation into a casteless fraternity of the Khalsa. Their Hindu names were changed and they were given one family name, Singh. The baptism symbolized rebirth, by which the initiated were considered as having renounced their previous occupations and become soldiers. They were prescribed five emblems – unshorn hair; a comb, knee length breeches; a steel bracelet; and to be ever armed with a sabre. In addition to this the

Khalsa were not to smoke, chew tobacco or consume alcoholic drinks or to eat an animal which had been slaughtered by bleeding to death. Having initiated the five Sikhs, the Guru asked them to baptise him into the new fraternity. The Guru was no longer their superior; he had merged his entity in the Khalsa (Singh, 2004 pp. 85).

For the Sikh community in Punjab, the Gurdwara plays a pivotal role. It is a focal point for all religious, cultural and educational activities. The whole community would gather at the monthly celebrations, important religious occasions, births, deaths and weddings. On important occasions, of either adversity or a visit by an important person, the community would gather at the Gurdwara. The author's first fourteen years of life were spent in a village, populated by refugee Sikh farmers, uprooted from what became Pakistan. They were allocated land and houses previously occupied by Muslim families. The village had a beautiful Mosque, but there was no fully functional Gurdwara until 1973. The other community in the village was the untouchables who worked mainly for the Sikh farmers, but there was no social interaction between the two communities.

All the author's relatives were Sikhs and he was brought up socially in the Sikh way. Family members did read from parts of Guru Granth Sahib and attended Sikh gatherings in other villages. The males in the extended family had grown their hair and the author wore a turban all these years. The author's father immigrated to England in 1954 and he next saw him after six years when he visited the family and stayed for six months. He was the first family member who had cut his hair and, on joining his father in England in 1964, the author cut his hair also and removed his turban. In the 1960s there were very few Sikhs in the local community where we lived.

Since its birth over the 500 years ago, the Sikh way of life has evolved. In 1950, a manual of Sikh conduct was published by a committee set up by the Golden Temple leaders. Article 1 states that any human being who faithfully believes in One Immortal being, the Ten Gurus, The Guru Granth Sahib, the utterances and teachings of the Gurus, the Baptism bequeathed by the Tenth Guru, and who does not owe allegiance to any other religion is a Sikh (McLeod, 1997, pp 450). The daily routine requires that a Sikh will rise at dawn and after taking a bath will meditate by reciting hymns composed by Guru Nanak and Guru Gobind Sahib. Next at sunset, a follower will recite the Rahiras and before going to bed, will repeat a prayer called Sohilla.

In modern India, the Sikh community has been politicized and the main party Akali Dal controls the main Sikh shrines and is responsible for providing religious guidance. The recent separatist movement for an independent homeland for the Sikhs has polarised the Sikh community, at home and abroad. In the Gurdwaras controlled by the militants, people take the communal meal sitting on the floor while in those under moderates' control normally people use tables and chairs. What has been previously discussed is the Sikh way of life which has evolved mainly for the Sikh farming community living in Punjab. In England the author has studied and mixed with followers of many religious traditions and thought systems. One of these influences was the trade union movement and progressive organisations, like the Indian Workers Association (IWA) of Great Britain. The IWA presented an analysis of society in terms of the class system and religion was seen only to divide and to control the ordinary people.

During his university days, the author experienced a liberal education which encouraged the study and exploration of new ideas. The English environment also provided opportunities to mix socially with Muslims, Hindus and Christians. The present religious studies course has provided a platform for reflection and discussion.

According to McLeod (1998), the Sikh way of life can be divided into a number of traditions. The adoption of the Khalsa tradition and the associated baptism has limited relevance in a society where the freedom to religious practice is enshrined in law. One can be a Sikh, without the outward symbols of the faith (Gatrad, et al, 2005). The author practises the core teachings of the Gurus, including prayer, belief in equality, and service to the community. My belief in one eternal God, the ten Gurus and accepting the Guru Granth Sahib as the eternal Guru, leads me to the conclusion that I am moving closer to becoming a proud member of the Sikh family.

References:
Gatrad, A.R. et al. (eds) (2005), Palliative Care for South Asians: Muslims, Hindus and Sikhs, London: Quay Books.
Jhutti-Johal, J. (2011), Sikhism Today, Continum International Publishing Group, London.
McLeod, H. (1998), The Sikh Tradition, (ed.) Beckerlegge, G. in The World Religions Reader, Routledge, London.
Singh, K. (2004), A History of the Sikhs, Volume I: 1469-1839, Oxford University Press, New Delhi.

# Richard Stewart:

## Twenty years a Quaker

I have been attending the Ipswich Quakers for over twenty years but despite that length of time I am still an Attender, having so far never applied for membership. Quakers, or Friends, as they are sometimes called, are a very broad church, ranging from those with little Biblical belief to others like myself whose religious faith is deeply rooted in Christianity. I try to base my everyday physical and spiritual life on the actions and sayings of Jesus in the four gospels. My faith is essentially simplistic; if God created the world then his power can easily embrace the Virgin Birth, miracles of Jesus, Resurrection and Ascension.

In answer to those who cannot believe in a god who allows dreadful events to occur, without divine intervention, I believe our world is an incredibly beautiful place, we have been given self-will, which can be used for good or evil, and that many natural disasters are the result of our own misguided and short-term actions. Recent tsunamis caused most destruction where mangrove swamps, natural dissipating agents reducing the power of high waves, had been removed.

Every day my religious faith is expressed with grace before each meal, reading a Bible passage after breakfast and prayers last thing at night. Anyone reading this may wonder why I don't go to services of mainstream religions but I have found these too regimented in their procedures and trappings. With Friends there is no priesthood or order of service. The Meeting Room is bare except for chairs usually in a circle and a central table with a bunch of flowers plus a few, mainly religious, books.

I find the deeply gathered spiritual silence, and the 'moving of the spirit' ministry that it often produces, to be the best form of religious worship I have found. I also implicitly believe there is 'that of God' in everyone who has ever entered our world, from Adolf Hitler to Mother Teresa. Quakers also utterly reject wars and armed conflicts and I have over many years given personal testimony to this belief by involvement in marches against war, giving public speeches, and having any articles and poems published on this subject. This belief would put me at odds with many mainstream religions who accept the principle of a "just war". I cannot do that, simply because I cannot imagine Jesus Christ using a bayonet or machine gun to kill anyone.

# Rose Norgate: A Bahá'í in Beccles

## Part 1 – Beccles 1995

I'd like to introduce myself. I'm married, and have been for 26 years. I have two teenage children, the older a girl and the younger a boy. Our family has recently undergone a shift of responsibilities, as I have returned to full time work as a speech and language therapist, after years of working part time, and my husband has liberated himself from the factory job which was slowly grinding him down. We are both from strongly Christian backgrounds, but both joined the Bahá'í faith eleven years ago.

How does being a Bahá'í affect my day-to-day life in Suffolk? Well, actually it often seems to take me out of Suffolk, but we'll come to that later.

Day by day, I try to keep up the practice of morning and evening prayer, and reading from the Bahá'í writings. How much or how little time I spend, and exactly what I choose to read is up to me  it doesn't need to be a lot. There is a short obligatory prayer to be said in the middle of the day, which helps to bring you back to the centre from the distractions of the day, but which I've personally had great difficulty in remembering to say.

Bahá'u'lláh's teachings, on which I try to base my life, are not only spiritual, but political, in the sense that they tell us how to organise our community life in such a way that, bit by bit, we can create the "new heaven and the new earth" referred to in the Bible, and bring about the fulfilment of the prayer "Thy kingdom come, on earth as it is in heaven", which many of us have said so many times.

The Bahá'í faith is perhaps unique in that the administration is part of the revelation, and to be an active part of it is a spiritual obligation for Bahá'ís. In practice this means working in love and harmony with whoever we find ourselves alongside, not always an easy task, but there is ample advice and guidance about in the writings. For me, currently, fulfilling my obligations to the building of the new world order means accepting the role of secretary of our local group cheerfully, and being willing to travel to Southport in April as Suffolk's delegate to the convention at which our national body is elected. I didn't put myself up for the job, and neither did anyone else.

In the Bahá'í faith there is no canvassing and no nomination. All adult Bahá'ís can vote for any Bahá'í they consider suited to the task, and the person elected accepts the privilege of serving, if at all possible. Opportunities for service (a Bahá'í euphemism for work) abound in the faith, and there are always jobs to be done.

I teach a children's class, try to remember the refreshments, write letters, make cakes, take the minutes and so on, like lots of other women everywhere, while always trying not to let the fog of small daily obligations obscure the greater vision that attracted me to the faith in the first place; "—So great is the light of unity, that it can illumine the whole earth." (Bahá'u'lláh).

Unity is what the faith is all about, and the purpose that must never be lost sight of. I believe Bahá'u'lláh's statement that "the well being of mankind, its peace and security, are unattainable unless and until its unity is firmly established", so I take great pleasure in having been a factor in establishing a wonderfully diverse but unified community enterprise in Beccles, where about thirty people at any one time, from all beliefs and none, work together in love and cooperation to run a high street shop promoting justice in international trade, and a new attitude to consumption, and use of resources. The shop is now in its ninth year, and hopefully has informed and enlightened lots of people who are not readers of specialist magazines and so on about things they can do for the world's wellbeing, while offering them beautiful goods, and guilt free tea and coffee.

I mentioned that the faith has sometimes taken me further afield than Suffolk, often to previously unvisited parts of the UK for conferences and festivals, but to more exotic parts too. So far I've visited Poland, Israel, Holland, Kenya and Tanzania for one Bahá'í reason or another, and my nineteen-year-old daughter, at present in

East Africa, has lived and worked in Russia and the Mosquito coast of Honduras.

Why all this travelling? Well, the Bahá'í faith is relatively young (150 years), and relatively small, and its focus is unity, so the world family of Bahá'ís tends to keep in close touch, and as in any other family, there's a lot of visiting and helping out and sharing of all sorts. On our recent visit to East Africa, my husband and I took part in a very fruitful workshop where we British Bahá'ís contributed some finance and goodwill, the Kenyans contributed their research and practical experience in running rural pre schools, and the Tanzanians were both loving hosts and eager students.

It was interesting that our food in Africa was served by charming young men, and that the Kenyan teacher who came with us to demonstrate her lively teaching methods had left her three older children at home with her husband. This is not a common experience in Africa, where men see domestic chores and children as women's work. These were Bahá'í men, who believe Bahá'u'lláh's teachings that men and women are two wings of a bird, and that both must be equally developed if the bird of humanity is to soar.

Bahá'u'lláh stressed the absolute importance of educating women as a vital ingredient to the wellbeing of the world and the establishment of peace. Research is now proving him right, and the education of women is proving to be the most significant factor in the success of many social and economic development projects, particularly in the field of population control and child health.

Does my faith affect my working life? I hope so. I truly believe we were all created equal, with the capacity to reflect the attributes of God, and I hope I can be clear minded enough to acknowledge any prejudices that linger despite my best efforts, and strive not to let them get in the way. Bahá'u'lláh teaches us to look only at the good qualities in our fellows, and to act at all times with love and courtesy. It's surprising how helpful this can be in staff meetings and potentially difficult situations, if only we can follow it. Patience is easier to come by if you're doing your job for love as well as money.

My working life is made easier by the support of my husband, who combines keeping the household clean, comfortable and fed, with lots of useful casual and voluntary work, after a lifetime of being a wage slave for the family. He takes pleasure in service, and does not feel demeaned by his role, any more than I feel I deserve special privileges for being the main income earner. We have tried to bring our children up to be independent but not selfish, and to practice the habit of consultation.

In the Bahá'í faith young people cannot be deemed Bahá'í by virtue of their parents' religion. Once they reach the age of fifteen, they are responsible for their own beliefs, and can choose to register as Bahá'ís if they wish. My daughter has no doubts about her faith; the Bahá'í vision is what inspires her and motivates all her choices and actions. My son is still weighing things up, but I am pleased to see on his report that he can be a "moderating influence" in class discussions, and am confident that whatever he chooses, the Bahá'í teachings are a treasury he'll draw on all his life.

I'd like to finish with an exhortation that I'm happy to take as my inspiration, "O handmaid of God; peace must first be established among individuals, until it leadeth in the end to peace among nations. Wherefore, O ye Bahá'ís, strive ye with all your might to create, through the power of the word of God, genuine love, spiritual communion and durable bonds among individuals. This is your task."

### Part 2 – Beccles 2013

It is now 16 years on since I contributed my story to 'Finding our Way and Sharing our Stories'. How have I and the Bahá'í faith fared here in Suffolk over that time?

Well, I'm still here trying to be a Bahá'í and still with my husband of 42 years. The children have moved on and I now have a lovely son-in-law and two bright, healthy grandchildren. My daughter, who at the last time of writing was actively serving with the Bahá'í community in East Africa, went on to university where she took an active role in Bahá'í activities while making the most of all the opportunities of life in Cambridge. The next steps were work in management consultancy (a far cry from living in a humble hut in rural Kenya, in terms of lifestyle), followed by a return to university to take up a PhD in immunology. This period saw her beginning to question her faith, and after much soul-searching, she decided she was an atheist. My son never made the decision to declare himself a Bahá'í and probably never will – he is not a "joiner" – but he is strongly motivated by the Bahá'í focus on unity, which for him, meant bringing together the diverse communities around the cellar club he loved in Bristol, and fostering the belief that a good time was about the company and the music that they shared, rather than how much alcohol was downed. He feels that labels are divisive, and that's an opinion I can respect.

Following on from our own and our daughter's stays in Tanzania, we were very anxious to continue to support that community's efforts to improve opportunities for quality early years education. There already existed an inspirational handbook for anyone wanting to set up a kindergarten in an African setting with minimal resources and no formal training – the Yellow Book. This was the product of work done by a committee formed at the request of the world authority of the faith and had received great acclaim from many directions, but being in English, didn't easily transfer to Tanzania. We set ourselves the task of raising the money to fund its translation to, and production in, Swahili. This project proved frustrating in the time it took, and if we hadn't seen the situation in Tanzania at first hand we may have lost patience, but knowing how few people had the skills required for the work and how incredibly overstretched they were, we could wait, and eventually it was achieved.

Another wonderful outcome of our visit to East Africa was that we were able to facilitate a visit here, to our local early years settings, for a wonderful Tanzanian woman we'd got to know. By a combination of vision, determination and serendipity (or answer to prayer, depending on your point of view), Ruth had acquired a piece of land on which to build a school in Tabora, Tanzania, and had engaged a team from Edinburgh university's charity HELP, to start building it. I felt sure she was strong enough to take from our system what would be of value in her situation, and not be overcome by the sheer mass of "stuff" everywhere. I was right, fortunately, and the visit was wonderfully enriching for her and all the folk she met. People and institutions were extremely generous with ideas and resources and she returned to make great use of it all. She has now established a second school, and runs regular training days throughout East Africa to share her knowledge and experience, so our original small fund of £500 is bearing much fruit, and is a reminder that to do something is always better than to do nothing, and that we often have no idea what we're starting.

Back on home turf the Bahá'í community has been sorely challenged. Due to boundary changes, when the administrative areas for the faith were aligned with local election wards, we lost our 'local spiritual assembly', the elected group of 9 adults in one administrative area, which is the basic building block of the Bahá'í administrative system. From the time of our becoming Bahá'ís we had been members of the assembly and the discipline of a regular meeting schedule and the focus that comes from a group with a common purpose had underpinned our lives as Bahá'ís. What had been a cohesive group now dispersed into ones and twos and we struggled to find a new way, which would both maintain a sense of community but also, in the spirit of the change, enable us all to focus on our own small patches.

This had wider ramifications, too, as the Waveney Assembly had been a key element in the functioning of the faith in Suffolk, and we were left with only one assembly, in Ipswich, and that beset by problems of ill health, poverty of resources and other difficulties. These difficulties probably contributed to my husband's decision to withdraw from membership of the Bahá'í faith; always a rather reluctant attendee of meetings, and not drawn to study of the text, he was relieved to follow our daughter in leaving behind the formal commitments of membership. In an odd way, this was a relief to me, because he had been unhappy about his situation for some time, so unable to be truly supportive of my efforts for the faith, whereas since he clarified his own position, he can now offer practical help and support from a straightforward standpoint of a loving partner. He continues to live a life of selfless practical service to individuals and to the community – I like to think he's done the theory and is now doing the practice!

Despite the setbacks, the years since I last wrote have witnessed some times of wonderful inspiration and pride of achievement. Our local Bahá'í community is very rich in artistic talent of all kinds, and when it is all put together "to the glory of God" extraordinary things happen. One was the creation of a walk through experience designed to bring home to Bahá'ís some aspects of the life of the Founder Prophet, Bahá'u'lláh.

This powerful tool was devised and built in a barn just outside Beccles, with the help of visiting Bahá'ís who would come and contribute their skills for the love of the work. It travelled to Liverpool, where it was installed in the library of the university for the duration of a special commemorative Bahá'í convention. The powerful effects of the journey through the pitch dark damp "prison cell" with its heavy chains, to emerge into the orange blossom perfumed air and the sound of a trickling fountain in the final "garden" were far greater than we could have anticipated and for many, it was an emotional experience they will never forget. Our artistic fellow believers continue to use their arts, whether dance, painting, poetry or music, to illustrate the stories and teachings of the faith. One devoted Bahá'í in mid Suffolk has recently taken on the major task of producing a monthly newsletter for all the Bahá'ís of Suffolk, active or not, and this is already proving to be a powerful took in reenergizing isolated believers and strengthening our sense of community.

Unfortunately I am not an artist of any sort, so I have to make my contribution in more prosaic ways. Looking always towards unity, and building bridges between people, I volunteered to be a local organizer for SIFRE, which has proved to be a much greater commitment than I imagined, but also more wide reaching. It has brought me into contact with lots of interesting folk, and taught me the beauty of the developing story of religious revelation and practice. The Bahá'í teaching, that the teacher learns more than the student, is certainly true when I'm asked to share my understanding of the teachings of my faith in all sorts of different contexts. Interfaith activities are a very natural service arena for a Bahá'í, believing as we do that all religions are manifestations of the same truth, and all the revealers of them are of equal station. Bahá'u'lláh gave us very clear instructions to "consort in fragrance with all men of religion" (and women and children too, I'm sure!).

During my time as a speech and language therapist within a Sure Start team, I enrolled on SIFRE's new Diversity module, which ran as a Cambridge extra-mural study course. The course offered me many insights I would not have accessed easily on my own, and took me to places I would not have gone alone. For my research project I chose to explore the experience of mothers who had themselves grown up elsewhere in the world, as they tried to bring their own children up in Lowestoft. This provided an interesting conjunction of work and study, and was valued by the project manager. On the domestic front, my husband and I decided to offer ourselves as hosts for HOST, an organization that enables overseas students to spend a weekend with an English family, to get a taste of home life that can't be found in a college hall of residence. This too has been hugely rewarding and we have enjoyed every one of our guests and the special contribution they have made to our knowledge and understanding of the world. It's a privilege to be able to offer hospitality to some of these youngsters who have worked unbelievably hard, often in very trying circumstances, to get the opportunity to study here in the UK, and to see our culture through their eyes can be very enlightening.

2011 finds me retired from paid employment. My new role as grandma gives life another dimension, and my freedom from the clock means I can respond cheerfully to my elderly mum's requests for lifts or gardening. I've somehow taken on the responsibility for the catering at our local community-run lido, and I offer some informal English lessons to a young mum tied to home with her twin babies and lack of language skills, so time doesn't hang heavy on my hands. I continue to offer a monthly Tranquil Evening of readings and music from all inspirational sources and try to maintain the pattern of Bahá'í life in our small community.

There are times when it looks like an attractive option to belong to a faith where there are paid clergy to keep things going!

Like everything in life, the Bahá'í faith throws up challenges, and there are aspects of it I sometimes struggle with. Disappointment about the local situation of the faith can make it difficult to remember the beauty of the teachings that drew me to it or doubt their efficacy, but I don't usually have to look far for confirmation, and I know that, like everything else in life, it gives back in relation to what I put in. Abdu'l Bahá, son of the prophet Bahá'u'llah advised those who sought faith to "act as though you have it" and watch the outcome – good practical advice, I find!

*first published (part 1) in Finding our Way and Sharing our Stories (SIFRE 1994)*

# Rumana Zuberi: A Muslim woman in Britain

I was born in Blackburn, Lancashire, in 1962. Although I have lived in the UK for the past fourteen years my formative years were spent in Bangladesh. In fact the best way to describe me would be as a product of the East and the West.

## Background

I always acknowledge my Bangladeshi background when asked about my ethnic origin, otherwise I consider myself a British national. Unlike the majority of immigrants from Bangladesh, my parents did not come to the UK for economic reasons. Rather, acquiring a good education was the goal. Originally they had come to the UK in the late fifties so that my father could obtain his MRCP (Member of Royal College of Physicians) degree. They afterwards returned to the former East Pakistan in the mid-sixties. However, they decided to come back to the UK in the early Eighties so that their three daughters could benefit from the education system.

Both my parents are practising Muslims. They come from upper middle class families with long standing common interests in education and religion. Both families were land owners for many generations, but by the beginning of this century were able to recognise that the future lay in education rather than inherited wealth. Perhaps more surprisingly, against the background of the Indian subcontinent where women are only recently beginning to enjoy some equality with men, the importance of educating and encouraging independence in the female members of the family was understood early on by my great grandfathers. Later on the two families also shared the experience of migrating to the former East Pakistan from India after the partition in 1947.

My maternal great grandfather, a medical doctor who was awarded an OBE, employed governesses in the 1920s to educate his daughters and sent them to convent schools. In the late 1950s my maternal grandfather, a judge with experience of the Supreme Court of Pakistan, endorsed my mother's wish to become a medical doctor; a dream which was later realised with the help and support of my father, himself a doctor. Similarly, despite the premature death of my paternal grandfather in 1945, a Secretary of Bengal Legislative Assembly during his lifetime, all three of his daughters continued and completed university education at the encouragement of their brothers and husbands. The daughters in law of the two families are also without exception university educated.

## First Life (1981 1986)

My mother returned to the UK in 1981 followed by my father the next year, because the political instability in Bangladesh had made it increasingly difficult to get a good education for my sisters and me. The significance of this move can be understood by comparing our life in Dhaka (Bangladesh) with that in London – especially in the early years.

We spent the first three years in a two-roomed rented accommodation in a rundown part of South London. Our main luxury was a 12-inch television set which we bought in 1982. Between 1981 and 1983 we did not receive many visitors nor did we visit many people, although London accommodated a fair number of Bangladeshis who were either relatives or friends. Our constant companion was a portable three-in-one music set which we had brought with us. We all worked hard and kept each other company.

In contrast, in Dhaka we had left behind a five-bedroomed house with a garden overlooking a lake; we also had servants and a car. Dhaka of course was also the home of my maternal grandparents, numerous uncles, aunts, cousins and friends. At the age of fifty three years and at the pinnacle of his career as the top most heart specialist in Dhaka my father came back to London to work as a locum doctor. After a change of career eight times he is now a permanent member of a GP practice. Similarly, since 1981 my mother has worked more or less on a voluntary basis at the Liver Unit of Kings College Hospital in London; although her work resulted in many publications in medical journals she is now in enforced retirement due to lack of funds for further research work.

My parents knew that life would not be easy in the UK but still decided to come. The only way we were able to survive as a family the harsh realities of the transition from Bangladesh to Britain was through steadfast faith. Throughout this period my sisters and I were encouraged by my mother to remain firm in our belief that Allah would provide and help us overcome the barriers.

In 1984 we bought a maisonette in North London. My father also bought a car around this time. Gradually we also started to expand our circle of acquaintances, had a wider social life and began to feel relatively secure both financially and in our outlook.

Throughout these difficult first years we held on to our Bangladeshi cultural and moral roots. We continued to observe family rules, for example, that only Bengali could be spoken at meal times (this was mainly for the benefit of my younger sisters who would have otherwise forgotten Bengali) and that all three sisters had to be present for Sunday brunch (we were allowed to go out on Saturday night and stay over with friends rather than come home late on public transport). During meal times we discussed everything ranging from what happened during the day to the latest pop group or fashion to politics and religion.

Unlike the majority of families from Bangladesh, or from Muslim background, my parents encouraged us to become self-dependent and allowed us to have an equal say in major decisions. Most importantly, we were encouraged to ask questions about both Islamic and Bengali ideologies so that we could understand and accept them on our own terms, especially within the framework of the Western culture that we were living in.

In retrospect, these family debates and discussions were invaluable. These helped us three sisters to place ourselves on an equal basis in our adopted society while retaining the basic values and principles of our Bangladeshi Muslim roots. Needless to say this constructive approach also created a very strong bond between my parents and the three sisters. It also resulted in a better understanding and friendship between the two generations.

However, the picture will be incomplete if I did not add that these years were difficult for my parents as they adapted their outlook and unlearnt many principles they had held sacred all their lives. For example, my sisters and I preferred to dress in Western clothes for day-to-day purposes rather than traditional Bangladeshi outfits. Additionally, their decision to move to the UK had been unpopular with the greater families and therefore difficult to be accepted by all concerned. During this time my parents were also under a lot of pressure from the greater families to marry off their daughters, particularly me, and received a lot of proposals of marriage.

Although I went along to meet a number of these prospective husbands, I did not marry any of them. (The greater family's advice of course reflected the traditional outlook of the Indian sub-continent that regardless of the educational status of a woman her salvation can only lie in marriage, motherhood and the microwave oven!) These years were difficult for the three sisters as in our own ways we battled to strike some form of balance between the Eastern and Western forces that tried to make permanent impressions on our young minds. And of course our discussion sessions did not always run smoothly and ended up many times in the exchange of angry words.

During this period my goal was to complete school and college education in order to compete in the job market on equal terms as a woman. In 1982, after completing A level examinations, I joined the London School of Economics and Political Science where I earned a BSc degree in 1985 and went on to complete a MSc degree in 1986. During these years I undertook many holiday jobs. These ranged from helping in a bakery, to working for British Telecommunications, to assisting at a summer camp for disabled children in Pennsylvania, in the USA.

My outlook and personality continued to broaden and be coloured through travelling abroad as a student. In 1983 I toured the USA with seven British counsellors from the summer camp, from New York to Chicago, Las Vegas, and San Francisco, enjoying many famous sights. Again, in 1986 my youngest sister and I backpacked our way across Europe covering the Netherlands to Italy to France, including trekking into Hungary and the former Yugoslavia.

These trips were inevitably done on shoestring budgets, but they painted fascinating and unforgettable pictures of other cultures and terrains on my mind. Although these experiences were not unusual in themselves, looking back I cannot help thinking that in the context of my Bangladeshi Muslim background it will be difficult to find many such parallels.

At all times, however, the desire to explore and experience life complemented and strengthened my faith in Allah, and my belief in myself. Throughout the first life years my parents gave rock solid support to myself and my sisters in both our academic and non academic endeavours, patiently helping us take the easy steps as much as the difficult ones. As a result one of my sister has now become a lecturer of Sociology and the other is about to complete a PhD in Microbiology, and I am a banker.

## Second Life (1986 1993)

After finishing my formal education I joined the Bank of England (the Bank) in 1986. It was also the year I met my husband, Kamran, and the year my maternal grandfather died. By this time our life in the UK had become more or less stable and my parents had moved to a bigger house. I had also begun to feel comfortably integrated into the British society. Although I did not recognise it at the time, the death of my maternal grandfather, followed by that of my maternal grandmother in 1988, started the gradual erosion of the special bond between me and Bangladesh.

The most emotionally difficult blow was struck when my grandparents' house, the house that symbolised my childhood, was torn down in 1989. From then on I could only look forward to a life as a British Muslim in the UK. Since my paternal grandparents had passed away before my parents were married, the bonding with my uncles, aunts and cousins on my father's side remained strong but could not stop the haemorrhaging of my special bond with Dhaka; as neither could the closeness with my uncles, aunts and cousins on my mother's side.

This turning point of my life coincided with the growing awareness and understanding of British society on two different levels simultaneously. Firstly, the Bank afforded an overview of the City of London (the City) as a major international financial centre; and secondly, following my marriage and move to Ipswich in 1989, I came to know life outside the metropolis of London. Both experiences have been invaluable and fascinating in their own ways.

I will not dwell on the workings of the Bank and the City since much has been written about the subject. Strangely enough though working at the Bank has reinforced the three As of my life; Activity, Affection and Allah. In contrast to the City, and indeed London, the pace of life in Ipswich seems very relaxing. And the community spirit still seems to flourish here, with many neighbourhoods offering a sense of friendship seen in bygone days. The open green space that surrounds the town, with the countryside only minutes away, adds to the charm of Ipswich. In many ways Ipswich reminds me of the life we left behind in Dhaka.

Contrary to the popular image of marriage within the Indian/Bangladeshi community, Kamran and I did not have an arranged marriage, as did none of our siblings. We met through a mutual friend, and became friends before considering and undertaking vows of marriage. I believed that it was important to get married only when I was ready to do so, and even then only to a like-minded person. As a result I enjoyed my life as a single person to the full – travelling, meeting both male and female friends, going to theatres, trying out restaurants – doing everything that any other young person would do.

Luckily Kamran has a similar outlook to myself and had enjoyed his bachelor life in a similar way. He was born in Moradabad near Delhi in India in a Muslim family with a similar background to ours. His parents also put emphasis on education and sent Kamran to a boarding school in the UK at the age of thirteen because his father's work with the United Nations entailed travelling all over Africa. Later on Kamran graduated from Cambridge in 1979 before joining British Telecommunications the same year. He went on to gain an MSc from Imperial College in 1986.

In addition to these similarities, we both enjoy having friends from across the length and breadth of society because we believe that people need to be judged by their actions rather than on the basis of their race, religion or wealth, and certainly the Qur'an asks Muslims to be tolerant towards other religions, especially those which have received the Book. However, despite such common experiences and viewpoints, I feel that the necessity of getting used to the dissimilar set of values and outlook proffered by Kamran's family and culture has been somewhat more difficult than integrating into the British society. In other ways, the long-term exposure of his family to Western culture has made it easier for me to continue to uphold my non-conventional values. For example, I have no problem wearing Western clothes at my in laws because Kamran's mother and sisters do so.

Fortunately, Kamran is a firm believer of the Islamic principle that men and women are equal in the eyes of Allah. However, Islam also advocates that men are responsible for their women folk. Although initially it was difficult for me to understand this dichotomy I have now realised that my husband's responsibility towards me does not exclude my right as a woman to live on an equal basis as a man. In fact it is seldom mentioned that the first wife of Prophet Muhammad (Peace be upon him) was a successful businesswoman who held her own in a man's world. I believe that Islam is a dynamic religion which allows the interpretation and adaptation of the verses of the Qur'an according to the time and the era. For instance, the Qur'an told us fifteen hundred years ago that Allah created man from a clot of blood, which may not have been understood until recently when science explained the meaning of conception to us.

Interestingly enough it was only after my marriage that I first glimpsed the British/ Indian lifestyle enjoyed by those of Indian subcontinent origin settled in the UK since the sixties and seventies. I was truly amazed to discover that one could live the life of an Indian while being completely submerged in the English way of life, but of course many people still continue to remain cocooned within the Indian way of life without much regard for the host culture or ways. It was also around this time that I first visited Brick Lane, Ealing Road and Southall in London. These places are not only the visible icons of the Bangladeshi, Guajarati and Punjabi communities in London but also perhaps the nerve centres of these communities. But my first visit to the Regent Park Mosque in London on an Eid day was perhaps the most impressive, as I saw thousands of Muslims of all nationalities and cultures meeting to say their prayers and to celebrate the end of a month of fasting (Ramadan). Since leaving Bangladesh it was the first time I had been in such a large gathering of Muslims.

During this period I had been often reminded of my mother's encouragement to look at the principles and underlying philosophies of Islam instead of superficially following the ways of a Muslim life. As a result, I tried to study the Qur'an and the life of Muhammad (Peace be upon him) with an open mind and I have tried to follow Islam as the dynamic religion it is.

For example, many Muslim women and girls in the UK choose to cover their heads with scarves as a sign of modesty and brave the cold weather in their native garments rather than Western clothes. Now, the practice of covering the head arises out of the advice in the Qur'an to dress in such a way as not to attract undue attention. Importantly, the advice is directed equally at men and women. But somewhere along the annals of history religion, culture and the concept that women are responsible for controlling the baser instincts of men (rather than men being responsible for their own actions) have merged, resulting in Muslim women either subjecting themselves or being subjected to restrictions not visited upon men. Therefore, scarf draped ladies are rarely seen to be accompanied by similarly covered men. Although I cover my head for saying my prayers I will only do so in a social gathering if the Muslim men present do the same.

Also, since according to my interpretation of the Qur'an I believe that I am allowed to wear Western clothes as long as I am dressed modestly, I continue to do so. Another example is that many Muslims do not touch meat or poultry which is not Halal. However, I find it difficult to believe that if circumstances are such that I must either eat non-Halal meat or starve then Allah, the Most Merciful, would consider it a sin if I choose the former. In fact I have had to make this choice many times when travelling outside the UK in other Western countries, especially where vegetarian food is not easily available.

Ironically, unscrupulous meat merchants in the UK take advantage of steadfast Muslims and sell them non-Halal meat as Halal, thus making a mockery of the whole argument.

By 1993, twelve years after arriving in the UK, I have become a moderate British Muslim without compromising my faith, values and outlook.

## Third Life (1994-1995)

The current phase of my life in the UK is as a mother. Kamran and I became the proud parents of a baby girl, Farah, in September 1994. We hope to raise her as an integrated British Muslim. Although we do not expect it to be an easy task we aspire to succeed. This is also the time when we perhaps really begin to understand our parents and appreciate the difficulty of the task they faced in bringing up their children. In fact, I believe that it is one of the hardest and most responsible task that one could ever be expected to undertake.

Since my third life has just started I am yet to face all its trials and tribulations and joys and achievements. But I continue to believe strongly in Allah and Islam and I hope to have the strength to overcome all difficulties and teach Farah to do the same. I have realised, however, that the rat race starts before babies even get out of their nappies!

## Comment:

I believe that there are many moderate, i.e. faithful but integrated, Muslims like me in the U.K. However, there are perhaps also as many, if not more, fundamentalist Muslims who do not wish to integrate culturally to the extent that Kamran and I and our families have done. Frequently the actions of such Muslims, even with the best of intentions, become translated incorrectly and therefore misunderstood.

In many ways the more fundamentalist of my fellow Muslims are in fact just trying to maintain their roots. Just as their counterparts from Christian, Jewish, Hindu, Sikh or Buddhist backgrounds are also trying to do, and just as the Europeans did a few centuries ago in countries they colonised. The main difference seems to be that following the end of the cold war Muslims find themselves being portrayed as the new bogeyman of the West. In fact the villains in many popular films and novels are now Islamic terrorists.

Of course international terrorism can never be condoned and I believe that blame should be given where it is due, but the reasons behind such desperate acts need to be addressed. Otherwise, the outright dismissal of perceived grievances conveys the message that only Muslims care about each other and must unite against everyone else; i.e. the bogeyman becomes a self fulfilling prophecy. It also turns moderate Muslims into die hard fundamentalists.

## My Story – continued (June 2013)

It is incredible to think that almost fifteen years have passed since I wrote 'My Story'. Farah is now taking a gap year, experiencing the business environment within a global institution whilst our son Sami will be starting his GCSEs soon. Although we are happy in our daily lives, unpredictable international and national events threaten to have an impact on our sense of belonging and acceptance within the wider community. I refer to a number of exceptionally tragic occurrences, including 9/11, 7/7 and Drummer Rigby, as well as the allied invasion of Iraq and Afghanistan, with their far-reaching consequences.

I believe that as a direct result of such events, the lives of Muslims living in the West have become difficult, as we are all tainted with the same brush, regardless of whether we are moderate, traditional or fundamentalist believers in Islam, or perhaps just only Muslim by name. Every one of us now seem to get labelled, and perhaps even more importantly, treated, as potential terrorists as soon as our religious identity becomes known. My plea to greater society would be to understand that the vastly overwhelming majority of Muslims only want to live a happy, prosperous and successful life, just like everybody else.

*first published in Finding our Way and Sharing our Stories (SIFRE 1994)*

# Sara Ali: A cry for Iraq

I used to live in the city of Erbil in the Kurdish part of Iraq. I left there in 1998 to go to university in Sulaman, where I joined the democratic movement which put my life at risk. From there I came to the UK as a refugee. I am now a British citizen.

Erbil is a city of over a million and a half people including alongside the majority who are Sunni Muslims, Christians about 10%, Yazidis and other small groups. People of these different faiths lived side by side and their children mixed with each other and made friends in school. A Yazidi family lived next door to us for a few years as my Grandfather's tenants. There was and still is no religious conflict between the people of Erbil.

In fact Erbil is a city to which people have recently fled for safety and its citizens were quick to give them help, before any came from the government or any foreign aid arrived.

My children who were born in Ipswich and view it as their home, speak English as their first language and are not very aware of what is going on in Iraq and the Middle East in general. However, I watch Kurdish TV and they see me upset. They know that I have had difficulty sleeping recently and they ask me why.

Of course, I am worrying about members of my family who are still in Iraq and I was deeply shocked when ISIL entered Mosul, another city with a mixed population, but most of all I was shocked when Shangal was captured, and Yazidi children were killed and Yazidi women were taken away. Many fled to the mountains. They were totally helpless and I wept when I heard their stories.

# Saroop Kaur (1924-2013):
## A tribute to a Grandmother

Our grandmother was known affectionately by her grandchildren as 'Bobo', meaning grandmother.

It was difficult to write something that covered everything, given that she had such a long and full life, and secondly because she was blessed with such a large family.

Bobo Ji was born on 13th March 1924 in Poona, South India. Her father's name was Pirmal Dass Singh Potiwal and she was the youngest daughter with 5 brothers and 4 sisters.

She married our Bapu Ji (grandfather), Labh Singh Digpal, in 1941.

Bobo and Bapu Ji lived in Islam Ganj in Ludhiana (Punjab, India).

Bapu Ji visited the UK in the early 1950s, travelling throughout England, Scotland and Ireland.

He then brought Bobo and his family to England in 1956 and they moved to 37 Emlyn Street, Ipswich.

One of the things we as grandchildren were interested to know was why they chose to move to Ipswich with Bapuji having travelled so much around the country. Unfortunately, none of our elders knew the exact reason. However I can surmise from this that the small town and the agricultural aspects of Suffolk were similar to what they had seen and been used to in India.

Bapu ji was an entrepreneur and, in 1959, opened a grocery store at 87 Bramford Road called 'Kashmir General Store'. The store moved to 15 Bramford Road in 1968.

At the time of her passing, Bobo Ji was 88 years old. She had 8 sons and 3 daughters. She also had 49 grandchildren, 67 great-grandchildren, and 2 great-great-grandchildren, making a total of 129 descendants.

I am sure that many of you here today have your own memories of Bobo and how she has touched our lives. She was a caring person and was proud of her family

The passing of Bobo Ji marks the end of an era, but it's important to remember that everything we are today is because of what our elders have taught us and the sacrifices that they have made.

Bobo was able to attend and celebrate her grandson's wedding in the last 6 weeks of her life in December 2012. This was the last event that Bobo celebrated with all her family.

We pray that, as a family, we carry on remembering her and remain united as one. We also ask that WaheGuru. (The Almighty) blesses us all with the strength to accept his will in deciding that it was our Bobo's time to make that special journey, back to the Creator.

WaheGuru Ji Ka Khalsa, WaheGuru Ji Fateh (The Khalsa; Sikh Brotherhood belongs to God, Victory belongs to God).

*By all the grandchildren in loving memory of Bobo ji*

# Shirley Smith: Why I am a Christian Scientist

I was brought up as a Christian Scientist, as both my mother and grandmother were Christian Scientists and I attended Sunday School from an early age. I joined the church officially in my mid-teens and attended a student gathering at the church headquarters in Boston, Massachusetts, when I was at university. Here I was met with such love and selflessness by all I encountered that I decided to become a member of a local church in order to be able to give back some of the service and commitment that I had witnessed in Boston. Since then I have joined a local church in whatever community I have been living in. I moved to Suffolk in 1972 and am at present a member of the church in Framlingham.

So how has Christian Science impacted on my own life? First of all I attended Sunday School. Here at an early age we were taught seven synonyms for God as given in the Christian Science textbook, 'Science and Health with Key to the Scriptures' by Mary Baker Eddy. You might say these are different interchangeable aspects of the divine nature, most of them terms directly or indirectly derived from the Bible. They are: Principle, Mind, Soul, Spirit, Life, Truth and Love. We also learnt the Lord's Prayer, the Ten Commandments from the Old Testament and the Beatitudes from Jesus' Sermon on the Mount as related in the New Testament. This was not just rote learning!

We were encouraged to see that these were important spiritual guides to our own lives. The Lord's Prayer reminded us to put God first in all that we did, to acknowledge Him as the source of all the good in our lives and as the power we could rely on when we encountered difficulties, setbacks or illness. We learnt how prayer included gratitude and affirmation of good, as well as petition. The Ten Commandments set a standard of behaviour consistent with a belief in one good God and the Beatitudes encouraged keeping one's thought aligned to the good. We learnt that our real identity was not physical but the image and likeness of God, who is perfect and knows no evil. That is the truth of our being and that of others. Anything that suggests otherwise we learnt to call "error", the opposite of truth and therefore not true. We could call upon these powerful truths, when faced with problems of health, personal relationships, schoolwork and life-choices. As we grew up, we studied stories and passages from the Bible and 'Science and Health' which added to our ability to govern our thinking and not to allow thoughts of disharmony, ill health or fear to invade our consciousness and make us suffer the consequences.

This was far from brainwashing. I was an academic child and keen to question assumptions which did not have good ground for acceptance. I was also a child who worked hard only at what I wanted to. I enjoyed Sunday School but I can't say that I carried all its teachings beyond the doors of the church.

However, as I grew older, I began to realise how valuable and useful what I was learning was! As I moved to university and into work, I found that consistently studying the Bible lesson each morning before beginning the day provided a solid basis for the day's activities. Thoughts of inadequacy, loneliness or overwork could be replaced by the reminder that I was governed by God, who is the Mind that supplies intelligence, the Love that supplies affection, and the Principle that supplies orderliness and control. And this applies not only to me but to all those around me whether they recognise it or not. In my teaching career I was absent through illness only for two short periods.

Here is one of the aspects of Christian Science which is particularly significant – if I am subject to ill-health, my response will not be to seek medical advice or remedies, but to gain healing by examining what I am thinking and correcting it. If I find I have allowed into my thought fear of contagion, results of over-activity or stress or prevalent information about diseases, what I need to do is to challenge these on the grounds of their inability to destroy my God-given perfection and replace them with what I know is true about myself. This may seem unrealistic but that perfection is an ideal towards which I work continually. I may not achieve the manifestation of that perfection in this life but that is what I am aiming for and any time I chip away at the suggestion that that perfection is contaminated in any way is a step towards that goal.

There are times when we need help in identifying what it is that we have let into our consciousness which is causing the trouble, and support in challenging it and replacing it with the truth of our being. Christian Science practitioners are people who are experienced in doing this and have a proven track record of healing. They devote all their time to helping people through prayer and can be called upon by anyone.

When my husband passed on a few years ago, I found that my understanding of Christian Science helped considerably. I was supported marvellously by friends and church members, but I also had a sense of being wrapped in divine Love. This was so clear that, when I saw couples walking hand in hand down the street, I didn't feel jealous or grief-stricken but was just so glad that they had each other. I had, and still have, a firm conviction that David is continuing his journey onwards, held like me in divine Love. I get moments occasionally when I feel lonely. Then I have to remind myself that I am never outside God's care and that there is a purpose in my life, for which I need to listen to Him to find.

Shortly after David went, I started singing lessons with a brilliant teacher. Much of singing involves physical effort and an awareness of how one's body acts. To some extent I need to take this on board but to me it is more important to think what I am expressing and why. If my main purpose is to reflect God's qualities in every aspect, then I can claim the agility I need because God is Life, the ability to remember because God is Mind, a sense of harmony because God is Soul and the ability to communicate because all of God's children express these qualities too.

On two occasions at the beginning of the year I found myself with a scratchy throat, which could have portended a cold or something worse. On each occasion I was due to sing with others in public events. Each time I reasoned "This is an imposition and I don't have to accept it. My true identity is not my physical body, subject to the limitations and discords of a material existence. I can't be duped by another power claiming to control me and claiming to be as real as good. I can claim freedom to express harmony, health and normal activity." Here are a few reference points from 'Science and Health' which I often embrace on these occasions to align my thinking with good:

"Stand porter at the door of thought. Admitting only such conclusions as you wish realized in bodily results, you will control yourself harmoniously."

"Take possession of your body, and govern its feeling and action. Rise in the strength of Spirit to resist all that is unlike good."

"Jesus beheld in Science the perfect man, who appeared to him where sinning mortal man appears to mortals. In this perfect man the Saviour saw God's own likeness, and this correct view of man healed the sick."

On each occasion I was able to sing in total freedom and whatever it was did not develop further.

Many of my friends did suffer prolonged and nasty bouts of sickness this winter. Unless someone were to ask specifically for prayerful help, I have no right to influence their thought in any way. But I do have a right, and a duty, to claim a freedom from sickness and distress for everyone in general. My understanding is that whenever I do this, I lessen evil's so-called power even in a small way.

When the bombs went off at the Boston marathon, all the Christian Scientists I am in touch with were praying earnestly as were many others, I am sure, to know that evil is not more powerful than good, that young people do not need to be duped into thinking that bloodshed is the answer and that those caught up in the bombing would find the comfort and care that they needed. It is not my responsibility to hunt down terrorists but it is my responsibility to make sure that there is nothing in my consciousness or actions that could add to, aid or abet violence, hatred or division. Another quotation from 'Science and Health' which came up in a Bible lesson sermon recently is:

"The Christian Scientist has enlisted to lessen evil, disease and death; and he will overcome them by understanding their nothingness and the allness of God, or good."

This is quite a responsibility. It takes an effort and I can't say that I always succeed. But it is a goal towards which I am working.

# Simarjit Kaur Sandhu: Sikhism, Love, Amrit

I was hurled into a loving, cruel world. The cruelty followed the loving, the loving followed cruelty and I swam, sank and swam. Sometimes I dragged my feet.

"The British, such politeness – what a nation!" savoured Mum. She admired the British finesse in really enjoying life for the here and now. Not worrying about what will happen to sons and daughters and their sons and daughters. She liked their queuing for things and the fact that they really didn't ask you for dinner on a willy-nilly basis. If they did, it meant something.

Mum is an assertive, charming woman, not the archetypal Asian female. She would have been the first Asian alternative comedienne in England. She's known as the life and soul of any party. I personally think that she and my entire maternal family would have been a troupe of latter-day Ben Eltons, renowned, amusing prima donnas who always have a story to tell. At the Gurdwara (Sikh temple) she's the first to start singing along to Kirtan (hymns), the first to tell me and my brothers Sarabjit and Harinderpal to go to the front of the Gurdwara and sing hymns. She's a true Kirtan agent. "Well of course they want to hear more hymns," she would exclaim as all I could wonder was whether the congregation were gazing at their watches or whether they were in meditative bliss. She would have made an excellent priestess, as in Sikhism she could lead the congregation. As a woman she could become a priest and even lead the Akal Takhat (Sikh equivalent of the Vatican), but she didn't.

As a family we would get out our table and harmonium (Indian musical instruments) and the like, a rebellious rock band, "practising" together singing Kirtan (hymns). Sarabjit on the tabla, Harinderpal singing with me, Mum and Dad singing at a distance. I sometimes felt sorry for our neighbours; thank goodness for the last few years they were Sikhs too. To sing Kirtan, is to lift the cobwebs away, for try as we might to live life perfectly – we're barraged, well I am anyway, barraged by throttling brigands of cobwebs and ropes.

Sangat (community, congregation) – how divine! My family were my Sangat, part of the same spiritual Sangat. None felt obliged or forced. It was as if we were all friends in a past life, and we all decided that we would be born in our final life as Sikhs in one family, to be together.

Dad is a true gentleman, never raising his voice. My art teacher thought him so elegant. Tall, broad-shouldered, with a snow-white beard and gentle eyes. He's always had an affinity to WaheGuru (God) and the world. He is a priest but living within family; he is a monk but not without community; he is a Sikh but not without humanity for all.

His sentences sometimes began "Sorry but ...." Typical Asian obsequiousness or Sikh humility? "Why do you have to begin in such an apologetic manner, Dad? We don't have to apologise for everything you know, next you'll be thanking Them for giving us air to breathe." "But we have a lot to be grateful for in this democratic country." I suppose that when I look at the human rights situation for Sikhs since 1984 and that Amnesty International have never been allowed access to the Punjab. I have to agree. But I still kept my self-protecting, all-identity seeking stance in life.

"Well I'll be grateful for things which are given to me as a Brit, this is my country, and the first thing we have to do is to stop apologising for being here!" Those were my self-liberated words when I was an adolescent. They only liberated me verbally not emotionally.

Before that I felt that I was on another planet. I mean Hounslow, Middlesex didn't amount to another planet but it may as well have been and I was the alien to this planet. Despite my mother giving birth to me in Hounslow, Middlesex, I didn't realise what a battle she had set me up for. To fight my neuroticism in thinking every white person really probably did feel disdainful towards me, was hard; to feel I wasn't getting in other people's way, was hard; to make myself as small and unobtrusive as possible, tall and broad as I am, was hard; to shed my skin was hard. I met a wonderful Sikh, my 'bestest' friend in life,

Hari Singh. He taught me years later how to walk tall, how to be happy. Hari Singh is a true Saint Soldier, he'd fought many battles, but most of all he would say to me, 'Take from life". He brought the beauty of Sikhism into my real, businesses, educated, so-called dynamic, so-called whizz of a life and I will never forget him.

As I say the world is cruel and loving to me, but it is cruel and loving to you too, probably. Or are you OK? I suppose I'm wondering are we all OK in the Transactional Analysis and Gestalt sense, "I'm OK you're OK, " well never mind, it's a great book. I suppose I'm wondering if I'm OK in the grandest sense of being.

I know I have dragged my feet through the tumultuous, rocking between love and cruelty. Sometimes I did sprint. I could have sworn I did. There were just moments of wild running, just wild moments of freedom when your spirit reaches and is connected with life and in Chardikala - when we can really dance through life.

My paternal grandfather, Sardar Hazara Singh, won the George Cross. Sardar is a title of respect to Sikhs, especially elders. In the Middle Eastern desert the cavalry resorted to eating their horses and anything moving. Because my grandfather was such a staunch vegetarian, he refused, and carried on fighting and living on dried grass. Ultimately when the supplies were thrown from the sky, they only contained grass seeds. So everyone, even those who had eaten insects and all sorts, ended up having to eat grass seeds. Hence my paternal family have huge voluntary streaks of vegetarianism running through their veins. Sardar Hazara Singh and his brothers, Mahant Bhagwan Dass and Darshan Dass, were great worshippers of WaheGuru.

My maternal grandfather, Sardar Budh Singh, lived in Pakistan before the partition. He was an impressive, humorous man with a great zest for life. When my maternal family became refugees at the time of Partition and lost generations of inheritance, they survived on a small cup of milk for tea all day, between ten of them. But Sardar Budh Singh was larger than life. One night he gambled his fortune of generations by just upping and leaving, with the clothes on his back, his children clutching a few rupees and name tags in case they were separated. When they arrived in India they heard that all the Sikhs they had known, who felt they could not leave their homes of so many years, had been slaughtered. I'm not sure he ever recovered from losing his dreams in his heart. But his character was so amiable and jolly that he hid his sadness. The neighbourhood would talk of my mum and her sisters who always appeared radiant with laughter. "What do they eat? Why do they look so good in cheap khadar (linen)?" their friends would say. They were always laughing.

Up and down so life went on until one day I looked into the eyes of a Sikh. He was going to drink the Guru's Amrit (Nectar in Baptism). He would belong to the Khalsa (Baptised Sikhs), be joined in marriage to WaheGuru. WaheGuru, the most beautiful, unbelievable power in this and in other worlds and lives. He knew he might never attain salvation. The very same salvation that the fervently religious talk of ruthlessly. As if salvation is something we have got front row tickets to just because we are self-ordained and we are self-proclaimed. As if we will all get there a lot quicker.

Once as I lay in bed, in Bonn, I saw the tree outside my window quiver. The leaves were whispering and dying to break free of the very body that had given them life. I realised that what Guru Nanak said, "Hukam Rajai Chalna, Nanak likia nal" (that nothing, not you, not me, not us, nothing can happen without the Will of WaheGuru), was true. Not a leaf in the world can move without the Will of God.

We can't even say "I prayed". Truthfully did I pray from my Bible, from my heart? Did I? Surely not. The countless times that the Bibles, iron rosaries encircled me, did I pray? No. The countless times I passed the churches, Gurdwaras and temples did I stop my car? Truthfully? Not if it wasn't in my 'To Do' list of the day or even in my Filofax!

Well no. If that were the case, the great I would have read all the books and journals in the library, the great I would have climbed many mountains, the great I would have achieved everything in life with ease. Yes I would have done lots more by now and I would have drunk happiness forever.

The fact is nothing, not even our remembrance of WaheGuru can take place without the Will of WaheGuru. We just make meagre attempts. We pick up the Bible, the iron rosaries and we sure as heck do try. No one has the front row tickets, because the irony is that salvation cannot be guaranteed to those who think they have a head start. WaheGuru is all-powerful and we the religiously or spiritually rich and self-seeking can be dethroned, dethroned as easily as those egotistical people we talk of who do not believe in His Name.

The Sikh knew drinking Amrit was just the beginning.

Anyway I asked this Soldier of God, whose enigmatic turban wrapped his mind wrapped in Nam (WaheGuru), looking into those piercing dark eyes, "Are you taking Amrit tomorrow?"

He looked away wistfully, "Don't know," shrugged his shoulders and walked off towards the Langar Hall (Open Kitchen). We went to eat Langar, food that anyone who entered the Gurdwara could eat. No one would leave the house of God, hungry – spiritually, emotionally or physically.

He wouldn't say yes he was taking Amrit. If he had I would have too, for he was a friend and a brother to me. I looked up to him. Out of love I would have drunk the Amrit of eternity. I was severely disappointed. It would have been nice to have had something to do tomorrow. I could have fitted in Baptism. At the age of 13 I expected to be a highly sought after item for all religions. My friend, my brother, the Sikh hadn't even sold me Sikhism. I really wanted to know if he would, take the plunge. I went home to watch some TV after the Langar.

There was no vision. There was no mind-blowing event. I envy all those who have such momentous inspirations. Surely you can question, or envy, but I'm being frank, I envy them all. But then I took the first step. A cold, calculated decision with no angels coming down to inspire me. But what I didn't realise was that with this first step began a passionate, momentous spiritual life. That my spirit was going to dance freely.

Please don't laugh. I honestly can't tell you if I fell in love slowly or whether it was quick. I wasn't sure if it was going to be just an infatuation, a crush or a life¬long affair, but my affair did begin.

"I want to take Amrit." Mum and Dad were worried. They were Amrit Dharis. "It's a big commitment." People I have met since that day, years later, who shy away from Amrit, tell me – "What a struggle! What a commitment it is. What if you ever put a foot wrong? Forgot to do your prayers? Forgot something, became lazy, procrastinate? Curses and damnation you'd be worse off than someone who hadn't taken Amrit but had carried on forgetting their conscience and themselves. A commitment that cages you...what if? What a terrifying prospect!" But I don't think they would put on hush puppies if they were climbing the Everest terrain of life as, beautiful as it is, it is cruel too. I don't think worrying about your sun tan lotion for fear of catching skin cancer would occur if it were a choice between sun tan lotion and a strong helmet or climbing boots. Do you?

My heart thought, yes, and sometimes your heart can do as much thinking as your mind. Come to think of it your soul can think too, sometimes.

My heart thought it is hard to love, to untemper your frail soul and leave it vulnerable to WaheGuru. But has the fear of failing ever stopped you from falling in love?

If it has stopped anyone then I suggest you seek out a good counsellor or a compassionate friend, what unhappiness! A good counsellor is like a good surgeon. S/he can reconstruct you, create beauty after the crashes your body and soul endures, drop pearls of radiance into your world, as mine did to me, but then I never said I was perfect. After all WaheGuru created good surgeons and counsellors too, so don't suffer unnecessarily.

OK, now you're thinking, well fear of failings never stopped me, thank you, or perhaps it was a sensible fear for your self-preservation.

But tell me honestly has it ever stopped you from wanting to be loved? Has it ever stopped you from hungering for love, from friends, companions, husbands, wives, children, parents, strangers, those who live and those who have gone from this world, from yourself, from the sun, the moon?

My Religious Education teacher at school, a devout Christian, had a soul that mirrored mine. He read of the ninth prophet's life and martyrdom, Guru Tegh Bahadur's supreme sacrifice in demanding the freedom of people to believe in what they wished and not be forcefully converted to the 'only path' in life. You see between us we had telepathy, spiritual telepathy. We couldn't see the differences in religion, culture. We could only see WaheGuru and God in Guru Nanak and WaheGuru and God in Jesus Christ. We didn't know how to brand our love even though we had taken first steps on our chosen path. For if you were to climb the Everest of life, you can't practise going through all paths, it would take more than a lifetime for that! And you do want to live a little too, don't you. All paths leading to the same goal as Guru Nanak said. We didn't think that either of us had front row tickets to Salvation. Perhaps we were stupid.

Perhaps the Reverend was madly in love with WaheGuru; perhaps I was madly in love with God. Ultimately each loving relationship is unique. You're unique so why should our love not be unique? Between You and me, WaheGuru.

I didn't love a distant Hegelian God. And I didn't care if WaheGuru was my opium, a great high and none of the side effects. The spirit of WaheGuru held me close when life crumbled out of my hands. When cruelty struck and no one could see my tears, the spirit of WaheGuru put sweetness into bitterness. The spirit of WaheGuru held me close, when life blossomed, and my heart began soaring. The spirit of WaheGuru made the world overwhelmingly contagious and downright beautiful.

But hadn't that always been the case? Hadn't WaheGuru always been there for me before I drank the Ainrit?

When I drank Amrit and breathed "WaheGuru Ji Ka Khalsa, WaheGuru Ji Ki Fateh! (The Khalsa of Purity is inseparable from WaheGuru and the Lord's Everlasting Grace prevails), "Amrit pulsed into my heart and into the same body that had been battered by love and cruelty. My head and ears tingled with adorning flowers, kisses and freedom as I knelt humbly, for once in all my life, vulnerable in soul and sat before my Love.

My Kes, hair, flowed in steely strength like Samson's before him and tingled in holy reverence. Never would I be able to deny that I was a Sikh and that I did not know or love WaheGuru. I would help others in the fight against cruelty, and never could I become someone else to suit myself as Peter (New Testament) betrayed the world. Never would I be able to denounce that I loved the Ten Masters and that I loved the Guru Granth Sahib as my only Master and Guru that lived with me in this world. Never would I be able to deny WaheGuru was my true friend in life.

My Kirpan clung beside me as a force in life. Saint Soldier. I wouldn't be a coward for others, nor for myself. My conscience would be as steely and strong as the force within my Kirpan, for WaheGuru is the strength of us all.

My Kacchara would allow me to be freed from a world obsessed with feminine sexuality. It wouldn't curb my sexuality but free me from the syndrome created by the media, by the world. Are we as women sexy enough, are we beautiful enough?

Surely there is more that we can burden our bodies with, make us more awkward, more, more…. I would no longer be either a Madonna-like creature or a Whore-like woman, but be as morally free and equal in love as men.

My Kanga held my Kes, in spiritual braids, and cleansed my hair and feelings. I hadn't become perfect. My love grew each time I combed and brushed through my spirit. My emotions rejuvenated.

My Kara embraced my hand and wrist. WaheGuru would not let go of me, even if I tried to wriggle free from Him. When you're angry you want to wriggle free from those who hold you near to love. I don't know if it is claustrophobia or fear of intimacy, perhaps you've never felt this, in which case you can miss this bit.

My Kara, my ring of love held on to Me. WaheGuru holds on to us even when we're angry and upset. WaheGuru held my hand sympathetically. Her/his arm around me as I sat feeling pretty pathetic. WaheGuru's eternity and power could never allow me to waste my life away as the eternity of torturous lives before in some cruel Karma (to have to be born again after so many births and deaths). Oh I can hear you, who have not really come to terms with the philosophy of reincarnation, think, 'Oh to come back and to have a good time'. To come back! For us to be born again and again in some uncontrollable cycle, to have no control over life, to live through the pain of life and death as animals, as anything or anyone, any person, as part of the food chain, is to have wasted our one chance as humans to connect to WaheGuru. It is to be hell in every sense of the word. Because, you see, your conscience goes with you, as you re-live and re-die thousands of times and your heart becomes so weary (Guru Granth Sahib). Like Ryder Haggard's 'She' burning, alone, all those you love die and then you have to love again. Not an enticing prospect. But that's what would happen if we lived like animals in this life, eating, drinking, procrastinating and not nurturing our conscience, our connection to WaheGuru. Well if we decided to stay ignorant of our Creator then, well, our buried soul after the grave of this life is really lost. I suppose choice is not something we use well, nor the body of a human.

"WaheGuru you are my Father and my Mother in the motion we know as life" (Guru Arian Dev Ji, Fifth Master). I wasn't frightened of the future of this love affair. For WaheGuru is merciful and my Lord would allow me to grow on this path to love. As with all love it would be an eternally poignant, volatile love affair. But a love affair that would soothe my heart, an eternity when everything else crumbled away.

"Much too fragile to grip tightly anything I love. I have been waiting all my life to be loved. Love is a gift which the kind ones give me, not because I deserve it, but because such love as I need cannot last long... Noble passion is a virtue if it sustains someone like me for a few flying moments. I am a small thing with the soul of a flower, not of a man with its awful dead body, moral responsibilities... Though years have passed and my hair has grown grey. I still fall in love with many things. I definitely have come to the conclusion that the love of men and women is always a volatile affair; it is an inspiration which comes in flashes and leaves us half dead to ourselves. Every fresh visit of this angel, though rare and far between, makes us unselfish. Nothing else... This volatile unselfishness and that fascinating evanescent feeling for beauty is to me all the essence of religion and love". 'A Volatile Affair', On Paths of Life. Puran Singh 1927.

When life snatched from me those I love, WaheGuru still held on to me. When I sat all alone in the darkness, crying angrily, well where are You? It's strange you know, people always talk of God and Light. When I'm sheltering myself in some lonely but relatively safe darkness; sitting in a deep, dark cave of gloom, don't say "Oh look on the bright side" and don't tell me that God is Light. I say relatively safe because, well life's got to be pretty bizarre and shaky for you to feel safe only in darkness. I guess your fears and thoughts are veiled safely. It does not help telling someone crying in a cave that God is Light because if any of you have been stuck in a pothole, light is not one of the most obvious things that you see. So you see I felt all alone.

For if God is just Light and I'm down a metaphorical pothole in life, then where does that leave me? Not somewhere nice I can tell you. When I prayed and thought of all this life and light it still did not help, because let's face it, an ugly dark pothole is ugly and dark, period. So Light and WaheGuru seemed very, very distant.

But not long ago I meditated whilst stuck in my metaphorical pothole. It took a lot of effort but I thought I'd give it a go. I'd tried everything else from – well I'd tried lots of things. My personal ritual, call it new ageish if you wish, call it a love of candles, is to light candles. Those unfortunate enough to know me used to be inundated with such burning materials. I haven't a clue what they did with their candles or candleholders. My personal ritual was to burn small candles, you know the ones you get six in a box, in front of a metal Khanda (Spiritual symbol of Sikhs) in the hazy start of a day, Amritvela. In the gloomy winter mornings I love burning candles and incense sticks as much as I can, for surely a light bulb doesn't have the same charm! But this time instead of burning the candles in front of the Khanda, I burned them behind the Khanda. I thought nothing of it.

Now you may think me simple. If you do you can skip this bit, well perhaps you have skipped most of this anyway, and in which case I can ignore you. But aren't the most wondrous things in life simple? Shouldn't our devotion to WaheGuru be simple, not stupid, but simple? Yes, an intelligent yet simple love. Well something simple struck me. The Khandwa was no longer its bright metallic colour. When the candles burned behind it, the Khanda was blazingly dark.

I was amazed. I'd always thought, as I festered in my emotional pothole, that if the Khanda was Light and WaheGuru was light, it was light years away from me. Now I could see that God /WaheGuru was not just Lightness but Pitch Darkness too. I wasn't alone, I had the Dark, Dark strength of God around me. God is everywhere.

*This piece by Simarjit Kaur Sandhu, a former librarian at Suffolk College, was first published in Finding our Way and Sharing our Stories (SIFRE 1994)*

# Sue Hewlett: My journey into Humanism

My journey into Humanism was a long one. As a child, I was drawn towards worship in any form. I'm sure theatre was part of the attraction – I was a dramatic child and loved to watch the goings on at the altar in church. Like many children, I loved the idea of Jesus and relished the colourful Bible stories associated with him.

Once, in Rhyl, my parents lost me. We had been walking along the prom when we came across a crowd singing lustily to the strains of a Salvation Army band. My parents ambled on, failing to notice that I had slipped in amongst the singers. I joined them for quite a while before Mum and Dad retrieved me.

To my shame I suppose, I continued along the Christian pathway without question, was confirmed and married in church. There was a moment, however, when I was thirteen that troubled me for a very long time. My brother was killed in a road accident, aged sixteen. He disappeared from my life; I wasn't allowed to see his body. My mother was devastated and would never recover. My father, I now suppose, felt helpless. He had to keep going, which my mother saw as uncaring. She had always felt that I was Dad's favourite; she had lost hers.

I was allowed to attend my brother's funeral. I remember preparations that seemed odd even at the time; my clothes had to be right, things like that. I remember standing next to my mother and praying that this ceremony would help. I remember choked singing and lots of words I didn't understand being rattled off by the vicar. No one else spoke. I think the vicar visited us afterwards from time to time. It didn't help at all.

I became a primary school teacher and had to teach RE. I was uncomfortable doing it and determined to encourage the children to keep an open mind. I always prefaced everything I said about Jesus or any other religious figure with the words, "There are lots of people who believe…" Even so, I was accused by one parent of telling their child they had to love Jesus.

It was during the decade when both my parents died that I finally stopped to think it all through more intelligently. Like many people, I had a lot of guilt to deal with; a lot of anger too, especially with Mum who I felt had abandoned me. I became increasingly confident that I could find my way through the agony, confusion, bewilderment, etc., by sharing my experience with other human beings, by rational thought and by reading the works of great thinkers. I need to do more of it.

About three years ago I met Margaret Nelson, a leading figure in Humanism locally, nationally and internationally. I finally woke up to the reality of becoming a Humanist and how it leads to new interests, meeting people across the age range and so on. I joined Suffolk Humanist & Secularists and trained as a Humanist Celebrant.

Whilst I am not anti-religion and respect those who have faith, I do believe in the statement that it's possible to lead "a good life without religion." I might even say that it seems possible that the world would be a safer place without the divisions caused by religions.

# Sue Raychaudri: Living life as a Buddhist

I was born in Basingstoke to Indian parents, grew up in Calcutta (now Kolkata, India) and lived in London for a while before moving to Suffolk 14 years ago. My childhood was spent discovering Indian traditions, culture, food, heritage and especially the many religions.
I went to a convent school and so had to understand Catholic teachings and I was also influenced by Methodism. Growing up in India, in a secular country, we had to embrace all religions and it brings tremendous awareness of different forms of worship and so I was exposed to Islam, Sikhism, Buddhism, Jainism and of course Hinduism from my family. To this day, I still respect all religions and celebrate all festivals from various religious cultures, despite being a practising Buddhist.

I have always been attracted to the teachings of the Buddha and found calm and peace in the sanctuary of a Buddhist temple, stupa or monastery whilst visiting Darjeeling, Kalimpong, Sikkim and Bhutan, when spending my summer school holidays there. These places and parts of Leh, Ladakh in the Himalayan region practise the Mahayana tradition of Tibetan form of Buddhism and since those early days, even whilst in Calcutta, I have preferred the smiley monks at the monasteries to the hullabaloo of the temples. As a child, I always loved listening to the stories of Prince Siddhartha and how he renounced everything to become the Buddha, especially The Four Sights. I still love reading them and reciting them to my 8-year-old niece, Angelica. I have also loved learning about how Buddhism has influenced certain kings and rulers in India and brought about transformation in them and their kingdom, for example, Ashoka and his conversion to Buddhism and how he helped to spread Buddhism to other parts of the world and his legacy still lives on in present India (Ashoka pillar).

I haven't converted to Buddhism; instead I follow the Buddha's teachings in my everyday life. To me, Buddhism is not so much a religion but a practice in beliefs and principles in our own lives. It is a deeply personal journey I wish to follow – a spiritual belief and progress in life to live a good life and do good to the community.

I am committed to the 3 Jewels and seek refuge in the Buddha (the awakened/ enlightened one), the Dharma (his teachings) and the Sangha (the community). If I feel I am in danger or am extremely worried about something I say the 3 words (Buddha, Dharma and Sangha) and it gives me strength and focus. I uphold the Four Noble Truths concerning the cycle of desire and suffering and accepting the daily changes, disappointments and expectations in life. I believe if you train the mind and become aware of your actions, thoughts and words, you are able to deal with adverse situations and develop a more healthy balanced living.

 In everything I do, say, think or behave, I follow the Buddha's Noble Eightfold Path – having the right view or understanding, right thought, right speech, right action, right livelihood, right effort, right mindfulness, right concentration/meditation. To me they give me guidance to live life whilst I am at work, at home or being with friends and family or in the community and in the outside world. Just like the wheel which propels motion, similarly the teachings of the noble eightfold path propel me and give me guidance and structure in life.

I have a shrine with figures of the Buddha and show reverence to the shrine and make offerings of flowers, candles and incense almost every day after I return home from work. I may sit and reflect on the day's activities for a few minutes or may wish to meditate longer, depends on my busy schedule.

I believe life can be found only in the present moment because everything is impermanent and everything changes each moment. If you are aware of this principle then you are better able to deal with things and let go and better able to influence the process of pain, suffering and happiness states of mind. I prefer the Buddha's Middle Way (not too little and neither too extreme) of choosing to do things in life so am not a vegetarian (my body needs protein as I am a dancer) and I drink in moderation (so I do not cloud the mind).

I can also cite another example why I practice Buddhism and feel a sense of deep connection … my name Sujata originates in Buddhism as she was the person who gave rice milk to the Buddha after he gained enlightenment on that full moon night.

I follow right livelihood and work in the public, charitable sector and community enterprises only. My life is embedded in doing good work in the community and helping people. Apart from doing full-time work, I give my time and skills and volunteer in many charities in Suffolk as well as supporting various community events. I continue to give presentations and talks in various schools and playgroups in Suffolk on Buddhism and Living Life as a Buddhist. I met my fiancé, Julian, whilst attending lunchtime meditation classes in Ipswich and we continue to enjoy exploring aspects of Buddhism and its teachings.

I complete every equal opportunity monitoring form or a survey proudly stating I am a Buddhist and most people in the community seem to be aware about Buddhism, so I do not feel the need to explain why I am a Buddhist. I know many Buddhists in Ipswich and Suffolk and access different Buddhist community centres locally, in London or in UK or overseas, wherever I happen to be. I listen to talks and teachings and love visiting Buddhist places and architecture. I do not feel the need to attend a centre to practice meditation or go on retreats, as I can do this at home or just sitting in my garden – I want to train my mind to switch off, no matter where I am, as this I found was the most difficult aspect of meditation

I continue to access and embrace the teachings of the Dalai Lama … *"Achieving genuine happiness may require bringing about a transformation in your outlook, your way of thinking, and this is not a simple matter".*

# Sue Smith Jennings: The Goddess within

**Why did I become a Pagan and a Witch?**

For as long as I can remember I have always had a deep love of the natural world. One of my earliest memories is watching baby birds hatch in our garden with my father and twin sister.

My father was a conservationist in the 1950s before it was a popular concept, and many ridiculed his views about man's destruction of the natural world. My parents ran a village pub. They were excellent publicans and had high standards which were proven by the number of people who frequented the pub. My mother and father worked as partners to run the business, both utilizing their individual skills to ensure the public house ran efficiently. All customers received the same welcome, whatever their culture, including tramps, Gentlemen of the Road, Romanies and cultural minorities. At times this caused my father ridicule from intolerant village regulars, but he would always stand up for the rights of all. I have carried these views throughout my life.

On reflection I was very lucky as a child for I grew up along with my twin sister in a close immediate and extended family. My maternal grandparents were both still alive. My grandfather died 6 years ago at 90 and my grandmother is now 94. My paternal grandmother lived until I was 15. There were always cousins, aunts and uncles around. My sister and I were never short of friends to play with or get into mischief with. I was always very different from my sister. She was a pretty little girl in every sense of the word. I definitely wasn't. I hated dresses and dolls, enjoyed climbing trees, bike races, and getting dirty, and my mother must have despaired of me frequently, for no pretty dress stayed that way when donned by me! I remember frequent rebuffs from her for my wilful behaviour. But my sister was never short of a champion for I was very proud of her being a twin. If anyone dared to insult her or hurt her I would rush to her protection without thinking, which again brought conflict with teachers and my parents. "Stubborn" was given to me for a middle name   a title I was proud of.

From an early age I always went to one of my grandmothers or a very dear elderly friend of the family, Aunt Bevvi, for encouragement. They were always more tolerant of my wilful behaviour than my parents, and Bevvi actively encouraged me to follow my instincts and think for myself rather than follow the norm; to be non-conformist and question what I did not understand or perceive as just, which has developed within me a deep respect for the older generation. This eventually led me into my career in Social Services working with older people.

I was married at the age of 17 because it seemed the right thing to do, as I was pregnant. My husband was brought up by his maternal Victorian grandmother who doted on him. I had two sons. Surprisingly they have grown up as well adjusted men who are supportive to their partners, looking upon them as equals. They have a deep love of the natural world and stand up for the rights of all. My marriage was very difficult, and I tried to conform to the expected mould for 18 years and in the end left to make my own life.

The thing which sustained me through these years, apart from my sons, was my career, which began 18 years ago as a Care Assistant in an elderly persons' home. Through the help and encouragement of my sons, parents and colleagues I gained experience and qualifications which led me to become a Social Worker.

As a child and teenager I was a member of a local church choir and Sunday school. As I started to develop my own views I questioned more and more what I perceived as the male dominated principles, and I couldn't conceive why supposed peaceful religions continually argued and fought amongst faiths, and were intolerant of other religions. I feel our society continually supports a social hierarchy which appears to worship material wealth at the cost of self-expression and cultural equality. In the past I dealt with these issues by becoming a social worker. For many years my career made me feel

I was at least trying to do something on a personal level in some small way to address the balance and assist others. In recent years this has not fulfilled my desire to help our sick planet and those who occupy it, and this has concerned me more and more.

I then discovered Paganism. Until recently I had no conception of this religion, except to associate it unjustly with Satanism. To me the concept of Paganism is the old world religion, a dualistically equal faith working with the cycles of the natural world, in tune with nature and oneself, using the divine forces of the earth to make magic. The union of my positive, negative, intuitive and logical forces all combined together within the greater sphere that is the Universe.

Within Paganism the previously stated basic beliefs lead to many traditions which branch off. Therefore each person takes the path which they relate to. The traditions include Druidism, Wicca, Nordic and Shamanism, and their origins can be found in the annals of prehistory. I follow the Nordic Path, worshipping the Goddesses and Gods of the Vikings. That doesn't mean that I worship idols, but what Stewart and Janet Farrar termed "archetypal symbols which are ritual components of the human collective consciousness." They go on to say "Paganism's basic personification of this ultimately is in its creative polarisation of female and male aspects, as the Mother Goddess and the Father God. The Goddess represents the formative nourishing synthesizing, intuitive right brain aspects. The God the fertilising, energising, analysing, intellectual left brain function aspects." There are aspects of all these qualities within each individual.

In relation to the female the Goddess has three main aspects – the virgin, mother and crone – and within each woman all three exist, personified in the years cycle.

The spring represents the virgin. A time of purity and promise when the buds are beginning to open, the animals and birds are finding partners, the earth is fresh and green and we plant seeds.

The summer/early autumn is the time of the Mother, when young animals and birds grow, the fruits of the earth swell and ripen to be harvested in the early autumn.

The late autumn/winter is the time of the crone (it is so sad that this term is now so derogatory). This is the time of the elder wise woman, and for reflection, rest, preparation and wisdom.

All the aspects are as important as the others and are revered for their differing qualities: the virgin for her purity and youthful vigour, the mother for her child bearing/rearing skills and sexuality, and the crone for her wisdom, knowledge and teaching skills.

## Pagan Woman and Sexuality

Within Pagan belief, sexuality is not seen as a base instinct; sexual activity is divine and should be treated with the reverence it deserves. Within the Craft you are encouraged to explore your own sexuality in a positive way individually, with your partner or group. This doesn't mean promiscuity or have anything to do with orgies, but something which is very special. Sexual energy is very powerful and can be used in a healing capacity if used correctly. In many cultures, when a woman starts her first menstrual cycle she is looked upon with distaste and is something to be hidden. In the Pagan religion when a girl has her first period it is a time of celebration for she has become woman.

Women are viewed as having their own innate powers and energy bringing them closer to the Goddess through their own cycles in a religious perspective.

I am sorry if I disappoint you but it is a myth that witches' covens indulge in orgies of depravity. The case is just the opposite. Pagans have a code of ethics and morals which are high, for Pagans believe that every creature is special and should be treated with the highest respect. It is a Pagan belief that if individuals commit any wrong which may hurt others they will be paid back threefold, an excellent deterrent and one that makes one think twice before committing any misdemeanour. Our motto is "Do as you will but hurt none."

## Pagan Women in Worship, Family and Work

Within Paganism women are equal to men in many paths and senior within the group (coven or hearth). Women frequently (in some traditions always) lead the group in worship and teach less experienced members. Due to the support received within the Pagan community the women are not afraid to voice their beliefs or develop their public speaking skills, and there are many women who are well known public figures who are well respected for their knowledge. It is felt that both men and women have equal importance within the group, and bring differing qualities, but to make the whole you need all of the components. Women within the group take their ties of sisterhood very seriously, expecting and giving support to the young. The Virgin, Mother, and Crone are all equally important and they need each other equally. This follows through in all Pagan life, both work and home based. Pagan marriages are a 50/50 commitment. Pagan men are very supportive towards their partners, encouraging self-fulfilment and expression. The women are never seen as inferior or undervalued by their partners or group.

Women are encouraged by partners and group to develop their skills, intellectual and creative, in whatever is their chosen field. All within the hearth or coven, be they male or female, are encouraged to have a specialist role to benefit the group. Teacher, priest, diviner, naturalist, conservationist, musician, storyteller, etc., are all equally valued.

Parenting is seen as a joint venture with both partners equally involved and taking a dual role, which is interchangeable, assisting the nurturing and encouragement of the young to be caring self-fulfilled adults, in tune with the natural world around them. They are taught to question in order to gain knowledge and respect for themselves and others. Our religion is not 'taught' to our young. They are encouraged to gain as much knowledge as possible about all faiths, to question and to make valid judgements. When they have formulated their own views they are encouraged to follow them, whichever direction they wish to go.

It is sad to see in our society how undervalued the older citizens are, but in Paganism elders are greatly respected and revered for their life experience and great knowledge. They are looked upon as the teachers and wise women/men of the group.

## Conclusions

Financially you will not find many rich Pagans, for wealth and material possessions aren't as important to them as self-fulfilment and care of the planet. Pagans are aware that money is needed but only to exist on a mundane level. There aren't many rich Pagans but most of them are happy.

From all that I have written you may think that Paganism is an easy path to tread, but it isn't. There is much prejudice and mis-guided fear against us for our beliefs. Our religion dates back to pre-Christian times, but we are tolerant of other religions, who we believe are seeking the same truths in different ways and with different names. We are not devil worshippers, for we do not believe in the devil, so how can we worship him? We believe that there is a negative and positive side to all creation, and you need both to exist.

It is very hard work to be a Pagan and witch. It involves a great deal of self-discipline, study and deep self-analysis, and therefore will not suit everyone. We therefore do not seek converts. You must be aware of and control the negative side of your nature and channel it and use it for good, and to enhance and develop the positive. It has been for me an experience that has helped me be aware of me, and to love myself as well as others. It has enhanced myself expression and encouraged me to take up crafts I hadn't attempted for many years, like art and music (I'm determined to master that penny whistle!). I am also writing! I never dreamt I would ever have the courage a year ago to write this!

My faith has taught me to value each stage of my life, for I will soon be classed as the crone when my first grandchild arrives. I look forward to a time of cherishing and teaching, of love and laughter, and walks in the countryside, passing on my knowledge and love of nature. So the circle turns and comes back to the baby birds hatching in their nest.

*first published in Finding our Way and Sharing our Stories (SIFRE 1994)*

# Tariq Effendi: My Muslim experience

I was born in the UK but spend my early childhood in Karachi, Pakistan. I was brought up as a Muslim and followed Islamic practices without giving much thought on what I practicing and why I was practicing. For example:

- Why was I reciting Qur'an in Arabic although I could understand and speak English and Urdu?
- Why was alcohol forbidden?
- Why wasn't I allowed to eat pork?
- Why I couldn't play lottery?
- Why I couldn't take interest?

I couldn't get much clarification from parents as they always said that Allah has asked us to do so. As everyone was practicing religion every day and there was nothing to compare it with I just followed the faith blindly until I travelled to Utah, USA.

My first interaction with Christianity was when I met couple of Mormon students who shared apartment with me at Utah State University. They tried converting me into Mormonism but when I sat down with them and discussed Islam they found it very similar to Christianity. However, they had differences with Christianity which I couldn't agree with as a Muslim.

I then moved to UK and have been living here since 2003. I have learned more about Islam in the West than in Pakistan as I couldn't find examples to compare Islam with when I was in Pakistan.

I also found the answers to my questions raised earlier:

Qur'an should be read in the language that the reader understands for clarity of thoughts.

Alcohol is forbidden in Islam due to antisocial behaviour related to drinking and medical issues.

The fat contents in pork can have detrimental effects on health.

Lottery has one winner and many losers, money invested is never returned.

Interest stops distribution of wealth evenly.

As an international student, challenges that I had to face to practice religion immediately after I left Pakistan were no provision of Halal food, interest based student loans, and no information about Islamic societies. It wasn't until I found a Mosque that most of my concerns were addressed. I believe that universities should have a robust induction program for new students where close integration to Mosque or Islamic centre and Halal businesses should be included in the program. The presence of Islamic societies and activities in the university will make new students welcome to their new environment. Chaplaincy should have an integrating role for students with different religious backgrounds to work with commonalities and discuss the differences. All faiths should be equally represented so students can understand other religions.

# Tony Gibbings: Rooted in Catholicism

There is something about childhood and religion which is intimate, nostalgic and formative. For so many, religion is what your parents or grandparents did and what you grew up with. It can be somewhat alien to contemporary young people, especially in our high-tech, career-driven world. Being brought up Catholic meant serving Mass at 7 am on weekdays before going to school. It was also early in the morning because you had to fast from midnight before receiving communion. Those days of fainting on the altar or in the pews are gone since the 'dialogue' mass replaced the Mass in Latin and the priest turned from facing the wall – and God – to facing the people. However, simply because priests physically faced people did not mean that they could face them emotionally, but that's another story!

I loved being part of the drama of the Mass and also focusing on the Cross during Lent, moving around inside the church with the priest as we followed the 'Stations of the Cross'. And the Catholic Church is all about the cross – with its dead body of Jesus hanging on or above the altar for all to see. Being Catholic means not only knowing the Cross as the source of our Salvation but also being completely comfortable with this graphic reminder – so comfortable that few even mention it or ask why the image of a dead body hangs in every Catholic church.

The Catholic Church is all about the body – the body on the cross 2000 years ago, the risen body of Jesus Christ in heaven, the body and blood received during the Mass, the body of believers, the body of the saints in Heaven, the body of Jesus carried in the body of his mother, your body, my body, the bodies of the unborn – all these are one body in Christ. Dead or alive, past or present, temporal or eternal, makes no essential difference. This is why unity with the body is taken seriously in the Catholic Church.

In a way, unity is more important than being right. If you want to understand why the Catholic Church takes the stances it does on the issues of the day, for example, in its political stance against revolution or its understanding of sexual and reproductive matters, it helps to realise how completely seriously it takes the centrality of the body. A Christian friend of mine once asked "Tony, do you believe you are saved by the blood of the lamb?" I replied, "Of course – and I drink it every Sunday to remind me!" The Word and the Body are one.

I was born to an Irish Catholic mother and an English Anglican father. My father became a Catholic when I was 9 years old, influenced, I understand, by the Oxford Movement and Cardinal Newman. Certainly, unity has been a driving force for my father throughout his life and my father's conversion came as a shock to his father, Cecil Gibbings, who was Anglican Vicar of Longthorpe, near Peterborough, and it took some time for tensions in this regard to ease.

I miss my grandparents. They represent strong roots. My grandfather not only ran his parish but had an international healing organisation, with reel-to-reel tapes recorded in a caravan in the garden and sent all over the world. He was also a follower of Sufism, the contemplative tradition of Islam. I have his books on both subjects. Holidays at the vicarage with up to 13 cousins were a dip into English village life surrounded by devoted Anglicans. The vicar may have run the church, but my grandmother ran the village! The vicarage was a centre of the community, with churchwardens, the Mothers' Union and all the panoply of Anglican community life passing through. But, of course, my immediate family attended Mass in Peterborough, not in my grandfather's Norman church next to the vicarage.

As an adult, I have come to feel increasingly that the divided church is a huge tragedy in our world. It is one more reason, rightly or wrongly, for non-religious people to accuse all religions of being the cause of so much war and oppression. I find visiting ruined monasteries and even active medieval and Norman churches, which are no longer part of the Catholic Church, painful and avoid it where possible. "See how these Christians love one another" said the onlookers of the early church. So what went wrong there then?

In the late '60s, with all the resistance among young people to the all-pervasive military threat to our civilisation, to the Cold War, and its proxy wars in Vietnam, South America, Africa, etc., a number of alternative communities and lifestyles grew up, including L'Arche, an international faith-based community, rooted in Catholic France, but open to all, inspired by Jesus' Sermon on the Mount. Communities in India, for example, include Hindus, Muslims and Christians, all living, working and praying together. Like many movements and communities, L'Arche grew out of an impulse for real change and renewal within the world and the Catholic Church, set free to some extent by the Second Vatican Council, becoming a source of great hope for young people particularly.

For me, L'Arche was something worth committing to and became a key part of my faith life from 1970. The communities, now 140 around the world, with 10 in the UK, put people with learning disabilities at their heart and encourage us to share our lives with them, rather in the invitation of St. Paul in his letter to the Romans (12:16) to "make real friends with the marginalised."

I moved to Ipswich in 1995 with Hélène and our son Joe and we are a part of St Mary's Catholic Church in Woodbridge Road. I know people from many different churches in Ipswich. I belong to a home group at St Margaret's Anglican Church, have spoken at and belonged to the Suffolk Theology Forum. I have worked for six years in a company in London run, at the time, by Evangelical Christians and have maintained friendships and contact with many of them.

What drives my Christian faith, besides the depth of spirituality encountered in the Catholic Church, the Mass and exposure to the Gospel message, is the hope for real community within the Catholic Church itself, where it is possible to sit in a pew every week for 20 years and not know the people around you. My Church needs more of what

Anglicans call "fellowship" perhaps, and real experiences of communion among its people. We all know these experiences when they happen and we all, I think, find them difficult to create in our fast-moving, money-centred and entertainment-driven world.

# Topaz Ladbrook:

# My journey of faith as a young Catholic

Hi, my name is Topaz and I am 13 years old. I am a Roman Catholic Christian. I'm going to start off by mentioning that I wasn't born into a traditional Catholic family at all. My father and siblings are not religious in any way! They are atheists, which mean they have no religion. My mum however was born into a Roman Catholic family and had attended church from an extremely young age. She and her brother and sisters went to a Catholic primary school. As an adult my mum hadn't been to church for the last 20 years. Before I started to have any religious views, my mum, granny and I discussed religion. My granny had been a religious education teacher in a Catholic secondary school. This meant that she had lots of experience of teaching people about faith. My parents didn't want to pass on either of their views to me – and discussed openly that the choice would be mine as I got older – and therefore I wasn't baptised as a baby. I went to a non-faith primary school – although we were taught about Christianity. Although my mum hadn't been to church for a long time she still had strong religious views and beliefs. 18 months ago she decided to return to the Catholic Church, and began attending Mass every Sunday.

After a month or so I became curious so asked if I could join her one Sunday to see what it was like. I have gone to Mass with her every Sunday since. One week I saw in the weekly parish newsletter that they were starting some journey of faith classes one evening in the week. I told my mum about them as I knew I would be able to learn far more about my new faith and we decided to ask the parish priest, Father John, if I could attend. He said I was more than welcome to. On the first class I was really nervous to meet the other people in the group. The rest of the group were adults, so I was the only under 18 there.

However, when I arrived everyone made me feel really welcome and I soon got to know them all!

The Journey of Faith is a programme designed to help those wanting to become Catholics to understand more about the Faith, more about the Sacraments and more about the teaching of the Bible and Prayer. This programme is run all over the world. This programme is a preparation for the baptism and/or confirmation of catechumens (someone who is going to be received into the Catholic Church). Each week there is an hour long session in which there is time to learn, ask questions and reflect. During the journey, there are a few celebrations which take in place during Mass. These let the parish know who is going to be received into the Catholic Church. It is a very good way for the catechumens to get more support from the other members of the church. As well as the other members, each catechumen chooses a sponsor to support them on their way. The sponsor is a Catholic and will provide encouragement and prayer both for and with them. I was able to have my mum as my sponsor.

I attended these classes and started to understand more about my beliefs and the teaching of the Catholic Faith. It was good to be in a group as often people asked questions that I wanted to know the answer to and we all joined in. My beliefs changed from believing that there IS a god to believing in God! This was a big step for me because I had never experienced anything like this before.

One of the celebrations takes place at the beginning of Lent when all the groups in the Diocese meet at the Cathedral in Norwich for the Rite of Election. Each Catechumen goes up to the front of the Cathedral with their sponsor and is asked questions about what made them decide to become a Catholic. I was nervous about what I would say but found that the questions were OK – and I was able to say that I had attended church with Mum and had been interested in the faith and had joined the journey.

At the Easter Vigil 2013 I was baptised, confirmed and received my first holy communion. This is quite unusual as people are normally baptised as a baby, make their first Holy Communion when they are 7 and are confirmed at 15. As I hadn't been baptised as a baby I was baptised first, then received the sacraments of Confirmation and Holy Communion with the other adults on the journey. I was very excited about receiving the sacraments and felt very special on the day. The service was very moving.

Since Easter I have been asked to join the Parish Pastoral Council as a Youth member which will be great as I will have an opportunity to have a voice within the local church community. Mum and I also help with coffee and teas after Sunday Mass and we have made some lovely friends.

Joining the Catholic Church is the biggest step I have ever made in my life and I am looking forward to the future and the challenges and problems I will have to face in faith. Really my journey has only just begun…

# Umesh Patel: My passage from India

I was born and brought up in a little village in Gujarat, India. My father, originally from Uganda, settled in India in the late 1950s. He was a railway worker and bought a farm in India and made his livelihood from humble beginnings. Of all my memories, as far back as I remember, our family were relatively comfortable but not luxurious by any means. My grandmother, who I remember dearly, had a great influence on our lives. She was religious and superstitious but at the same time very considerate, kind and protective of her family.

From an early age we were encouraged to pray and participate in numerous religious ceremonies which I feel has had a terrific influence on my family. We were also encouraged to be kind to all living forms, from ants to street dogs and the cows that would walk around in our village streets. On the way to our farm we would be given food to feed ants' nests as well as grains to feed to birds every morning and leftovers to feed to dogs as well as grains to give to sadhus walking the streets. All I am trying to say is, I feel such activities have allowed me to develop into someone who thinks about all life forms and those humans less fortunate than me. This has been particularly obvious when I return home now after enjoying a reasonable standard of living.

My father was equally religious and in his way knowledgeable and he encouraged us rather than told us to follow certain ways. My mother followed the family tradition, as housewives did in those days. My grandmother passed away when I was 13 but she has left me a lifetime of memories and I am most grateful to her as I am a parent of 3 children and feel if I could pass on half as much I would be a happy parent. Since being in England for the last 35 years I have been through many different phases as there are differing influences with which I have come in contact. I feel education has influenced me to an extent in my questioning faith and beliefs sometimes. Having science as my education background, as I come across different explanations,

I have had to pause and think. Influences from society and different cultures have led me to question certain aspects of religion.

As mentioned, having gone through numerous trials and tribulations, I have found my religious belief has prevailed and I remain a firm believer in an existence of a superior power. As a Hindu with limited knowledge, I am fascinated by explanations that are given in scriptures and depicted in many religious serials on television. I would like to travel to religious places and ask questions to broaden my knowledge at a personal level.

I consider myself to be a Hindu with certain beliefs which include the existence of a God that influences the universe. I believe in karma and reincarnation. I have had doubts around the definition of good, whether it means being kind/considerate/generous or whatever an individual sees as being good. My upbringing and way of life has allowed me to progress as well as I have done and strengthens my belief, in fact reinforces my belief. I have raised my own family here in England and as the children have grown up here they have developed a somewhat different outlook. They are not as firm believers as I am. I believe in guiding and putting information to them and let them decide for themselves. I do believe they will be religious although not to the same extent as I am while I in my turn am not as religious as my parents. I believe as time goes by and people are informed, educationally as well as through other aspects, they question and like to have evidence about religion and different aspects of religion. This is not always in black or white so I feel people tend to be mainly non-believers. This continues until at some point something happens and "by hoping and praying" things turn out to be OK and individuals become believers. At least this is my experience.

I was in India recently and I felt a stranger in some aspects as I saw some practices which may be considered "blind faith". People in large numbers did things that gave them joy and had faith in what they were doing. I feel happy that people have means to express their beliefs and they do so in the way they do. This gives our culture a unique identity in the western society. Currently I chair the Ipswich Hindu Samaj and in this capacity I try to bring our small but growing community in and around Ipswich together as well as reach out and open up to the multicultural society of which we are a part.

I consider myself to be privileged to be here. I have been given an opportunity to be part of a multicultural society and I value all the diversity to which I have been exposed, enabling me to become, hopefully, a better individual who can pass on some of the good foundations of my forefathers to the generation to come.

# Sanjaya Martin Spettigue:

# A Thought for the Day

Looking at the past, and at the present, one wonders if it will ever be possible for religion to exist without followers, at some stage, coming to blows with each other.

The prophet and mystic, Hazral Inayat Khan, tells us that behind all wars there is a suggestion of religion. He points out that people think the reason for war is mostly political, but in fact religion is the greater warmonger. He is a Sufi Master, who brought Sufism to the West at the turn of the century.

Sufism is the mystical side of Islam and is one answer to frictions between religions. Whereas theologians in college want to find out the differences between, say, Moses and Buddha, Sufism wants to look behind all religions to find their similarities and how they arrive at the one truth.

Religion for the mystic is a steady progress towards unity, or oneness, and an opportunity to identify with the good and bad in everybody.

So often where religion is at the root of wars and conflicts, there is a particular focus on a holy place or building. The sacred Temple Mount in Jerusalem, where King Solomon's Temple was, and where now stands two mosques, is a holy and most sig-nificant place for Muslims as well as for Jews. Just below this is the Jews' Wailing Wall. The proximity of these holy places, in a time of conflict, suggests a tinderbox waiting for the spark to set it aflame. But Sufism tells us the old truths of the East – that religions are not in buildings, relics or places, but in our hearts. The God of my religion and the God of your religion is the same God.

Therefore, like Sufis, one could be just as happy to worship in a Hindu temple, a mosque or a church. As Sri Chinmoy teaches "There is really only one religion and that is the love of God".

*Sanjaya Martin Spettigue is Chairman of SIFRE. He was brought up as a Christian. Over 40 years ago he became a student of the spiritual Master, Sri Chinmoy. Martin follows one of the paths of Yoga which form the spiritual foundations of Hinduism and which have been found beneficial by spiritual seekers with other beliefs.*

# Reflections on Religious Diversity

All religions share a common root, which is limitless compassion. They emphasize human improvement, love, respect for others, and compassion for the suffering of others. In so far as love is essential in every religion, we could say that love is a universal religion. But the various techniques and methods for developing love differ widely between the traditions. I don't think there could ever be just one single philosophy or one single religion. Since there are so many different types of people, with a range of tendencies and inclinations, it is quite fitting that there are differences between religions. And the fact that there are so many different descriptions of the religious path shows how rich religion is.

H.H. The 14th Dalai Lama


There was a time when I used to reject those who were not of my faith.
Now my heart has grown capable of taking on all forms,
A pasture for gazelles, a convent for Christians,
A temple for idols, a Ka'ba for the pilgrim,
A table for the Torah, a book of the Koran.
My religion is love.
Whichever the route love's caravan shall take,
That path shall be the path of my faith.

Ibn'Arabi (1165-1240)


Spirituality is not merely tolerance. It is not even acceptance. It is the feeling of a universal oneness. In our spiritual life, we look upon the Divine not only in terms of our own God, but in terms of everybody else's God. Our spiritual life firmly and securely establishes the basis of unity in diversity. Spirituality is not hospitality to other's faith in God. It is the absolute recognition of the other's faith in God as one's own.

Sri Chinmoy

Let there be one community (of believers?)
Calling to good and bidding to honour, and forbidding dishonour

Qur'an, Surah 3, 104

The union of hearts and minds and
Freedom from hate I will bring you.
Love one another as the cow loves the calf
That she has borne...
Let not a brother hate a brother,
Nor sister hate a sister,
Unanimous, united in aims
Speak your words in friendliness.

Atharva Veda 3.30

When a man appears before the throne of the judgement the first
question he is asked is not
Have you believed in God? or
Have you prayed and fulfilled the precepts? but
Have you dealt, honourably, faithfully in
All your dealings with your neighbour?

Talmud, Shabbat 31a

And who is my neighbour?
The one who showed him kindness.

Luke 10, 25-37

**INTER-FAITH MEETING IS A LITTLE LIKE A DANCE
TENTATIVE, LEARNING THE STEPS,
TRUSTING, MOVING CLOSER
STRUCTURED AND TRADITIONAL
THEN HARMONIOUS, IMPROVISATIONAL
TRANSFORMING
AS OUR DANCE ON EARTH
BEGINS TO REFLECT THE ETERNAL DANCE**

# Cynthia Capey: An inter-faith pilgrimage

I was an only child. My parents mixed with everybody and my friends were whoever was around. I was an avid reader. Because my parents were very involved in the local church, I was too. I was always asking questions and soon realised that the clergy didn't know all the answers! This made me keen to study and find out for myself.

At high school I wasn't allowed by the head mistress to take Religious Education at A Level as she thought it would undermine my faith. Although I think she was wrong, looking back I am grateful. Instead I studied English, Greek and Latin, and was exposed to different ways of looking at life, including through poetry and mythology. I found these subjects thrilling in their own right and they provided a broader context for my journey.

When I went to university I continued studying Classics for the first two years and began to realise that my concerns and questions and those of my friends were the same questions that the ancient writers were tackling – what kind of society do we want to live in, how should we be educating children, are we free to choose or are we at the mercy of fate, are gods and goddesses responsible for our problems and indeed is there a God at all?

When I moved over to study theology for the last part of my degree I was not fazed by being faced with those same questions or by being exposed to the very rigorous debates about the dates of the books of the Bible, their authorship or their place of origin. I was far more fazed by the fact that nearly all my fellow theology students were men and all the lecturers were men!

Having to study parts of the Bible in the original languages made me realise that it is inappropriate to say "The Bible says" because it is not possible to translate exactly from one language into another. Hebrew is written without vowels, there are no adjectives and much of the Old Testament is in poetry and metaphor. Also it is important to bear in mind that the books of the Bible were composed in stages and by many different authors. Understanding of a passage may be increased by some knowledge of the original sources, of the context of the writer, and of the identity of the intended readers. We must be careful how we use these ancient texts!

What view of kingship should inform the translation of God's words to Adam – have dominion over the earth? Do they mean "rule like a despot" or "take care of the earth"? What does Genesis say about the relationship between man and woman? Chapter 2 says that woman was made from Adam's rib, as a helpmeet. This could imply that she was an afterthought and was to be subservient. The Chief Rabbi with his knowledge of Hebrew idiom has said it means that she was to be at his side, as a colleague and critical friend! Christians can certainly benefit from Jewish scholarship – and vice-versa!

There are special moments in all our lives which exert very powerful influences on us. When I was twenty and still a student I attended a conference in Switzerland for young European Christians of many denominations. During the week we experienced each other's various forms of worship and sang the same hymns in different languages. That in itself was an enriching and moving experience, but the main impact on me was a sermon preached by a Dutch theologian on a text from one of the Old Testament psalms, composed at a time of danger and uncertainty about the future (Psalm 31:35). The text was, "My times are in thy hands". The preacher explained that there are several words for hand in Hebrew and this one was not the protective hand of God but the hurling hand of God. In other words, religious experience is about facing up to the challenges of living with courage and integrity in the real world, not expecting to have special divine protection from pain and suffering. There is no hiding place! This seems to me now to be at the heart of Christianity and Judaism, and indeed of other faiths too.

In the words of one of my university lecturers, Bishop John Robinson, "Truth is Two Eyed". We need to see things from other people's perspectives. This was driven home to him when he went on a trip to India and was exposed to Hinduism. It was driven home to me when I moved to Ipswich and taught at the then Civic College! First, I taught Liberal Studies to day release apprentices which certainly opened my eyes. Later on I was given the opportunity to develop courses in Religious Studies.

The Civic College was a secular institution, and so the Religious Studies courses were open to anybody. Initially the courses were based on Christianity and those who enrolled were RE teachers, ministers, some nuns, theology students and also people who had dropped out of the churches because they didn't feel they could ask their questions there. Two students stand out in particular from those courses. One young man joined about six different classes but left when he realised that Jesus was a Jew. It transpired that he was a member of the BNP! Another young man, aged about eighteen, studying the New Testament, was a Muslim called Mojlum Khan. Now, many years later, we are colleagues and he recently conducted a research project through SIFRE on the experiences and aspirations of young Muslims living in Suffolk today.

At the College I was also able to arrange courses in Arabic and Qur'anic studies, for Muslims (and other interested people) by bringing over lecturers from the Islamic Academy in Cambridge. In the late 1980s I also introduced short courses for the general public which gave minority groups a voice – local people from different religious backgrounds spoke about what they believed and how they practised their faith, and what it was like to be a Muslim or Hindu or Sikh in Ipswich.

There have been sizeable groups of people of other faiths in Ipswich for fifty years or more and there were Jews here in the Middle Ages. The various minority groups who had settled in Ipswich in the 1950s (Muslims from a rural village in Bangladesh, a large close-knit family of Sikhs from the Punjab, a sizeable group of Hindus, etc.) had not been welcomed into mainstream society. Even Christians from the Caribbean had been turned away from most of the existing Churches.

The Seventh-day Adventist Church, as far as I know, was the only church in Ipswich to welcome these black newcomers. Over the years Ipswich has gradually been becoming more and more multi-cultural and multi-faith. There is a challenge to us all to welcome newcomers and to help them feel at home.

I spent most of my working life at the Civic/Suffolk College and this was where my inter-faith journey really took off. The research I did on the faith communities of Ipswich and Suffolk which led to the compilation of the first books, the friendships which developed, chance encounters within the college with Elahe Mojdehi, Muslim, Elizabeth Sugarman, Jewish, and Bhupindar Singh Sually, Sikh, and, very importantly, the self-contained premises which the college provided, enabled a dynamic grass-roots, inter-faith process to develop alongside the growing programme of academic Religious Studies.

In 1991 it seemed timely to set up an interfaith network and we began the formal process. Shortly afterwards, in 1993, it was the centenary of the World's Parliament of Religion and as local communities were being encouraged to do something special to strengthen inter-faith relationships, we invited people to contribute articles for 'Faiths in Focus in Ipswich and Suffolk'. This was soon followed by 'Finding our Way and Sharing Our Stories', a collection of articles by women. The process of writing these two books, especially the women's one, involved people getting together and talking about their lives and faiths at a very deep level. It is basically through these early personal encounters and the friendships which flowed from them, that we have been able to build and sustain Suffolk Inter-Faith Resource. It became a charitable company in 1994.

Both books highlighted the multi-faith nature of Ipswich and the women's book illustrated how different and interesting people's individual journeys are. You can start in the same place with a similar upbringing and end up with contrasting life experiences and stances or you can start on different sides of the world, born into different faiths, and end up in the same location and find that you can understand each other at a very deep level.

There are many different spiritual paths within the so-called world faiths and I have learnt that people do not fit neatly into boxes.

It has been a bad habit of the western world to categorise people into official religions with fixed boundaries in the same way as it has put borders around geographical areas and created countries like Iraq, which were not natural entities! It has been a dangerous practice!

Our situation within Suffolk College brought me into close contact with asylum seekers. This has been both painful and also enriching. The horrific experiences they have had before reaching here and the difficulties they face rebuilding their lives without their loved ones, are overwhelming. Then they are often subjected in this country to inhumane processes which damage them even more. I have had the privilege of helping a few of them, who, once the way ahead was open to them, have worked incredibly hard to rebuild their lives, and helped others in their turn.

I have met many people of different faiths on my inter-faith journey and this has changed me. The encounters have not damaged my own faith – they have helped me to go deeper and have reminded me of important principles that can enrich all our lives. Now, although I have been officially retired from Suffolk College for sixteen years, I have valued being able to continue working, in a voluntary capacity, with people of all faiths.

Some basic principles of my own faith have been reinforced from my encounters with others, most significantly that the Christian journey requires taking risks and going on in faith and hope, whatever the cost, with no guarantee of a happy ending! It also invites me to look outwards and to keep connected to the world, like the 'Walking Madonna' at Salisbury Cathedral, striding off into the hurly-burly of the city. This echoes a passage from Gitanjali, by the Bengali poet,

Rabindranath Tagore – sections 10 and 11. "Here is thy footstool and there rest thy feet, where live the poorest and lowliest and lost...."

I have discovered new perspectives. Here are just some of the treasures I am taking with me on the next stage of my journey.

- From Buddhism – the need for compassion, and to have the right attitude to every aspect of everything we do.
- From Hinduism – that 'God' is beyond description, and that we must not mistake the statues, symbols and metaphors we use, for what is ultimately beyond words.
- From Judaism – that it is alright to question our concept of God and that scriptures have many depths of meaning with which we must wrestle.
- From Islam – that true religion is meant to be a discipline that leads to a healthy body as well as to holiness and peace. Just think, for example, of the effect on the body of taking the Muslim prayer postures five times a day, let alone observing Ramadan, the annual month of fasting!
- From Paganism – that sacred spaces can and should be shared and that every season and every stage of life should be honoured.
- From the Bahá'í faith and Sikhism – that all paths can lead to God
- From Jainism and Taoism – that the whole of nature should be treated with reverence. That all living things are bound together in mutual dependence and that mankind has no right to control.
- From Humanism – that whatever our faith we share a common humanity and that every human being is worthy of respect.

These are just hints of a process of change and growth that has gone on at a very deep level. In my experience, an involvement with committed people of different faiths within the interfaith process does not put one in danger of conversion but can enable an ongoing series of transformations which can take the person deeper into the heart of their own faith to a place where rigid boundaries between faiths cease to exist. This transforming experience can be seen throughout the pages of the gospels and in many of the epistles, but it is also an everyday human experience if we are open to other people.

I have learned how easy it is for people of faith to fall short of their ideals or to lose their way, that religions can become so institutionalised that they lose their spiritual vitality, and that the teachings of founders, prophets and Gurus can be distorted and subverted by their followers.

I firmly believe that inter-faith encounters and the opportunities we now have for working together in a spirit of openness and mutual trust are necessary for the survival and purification of the faiths themselves, let alone for the good of society. If we trust each other enough, we can offer each other a loving critique which will help us all to be more faithful to our shared principles. These were summed up in the Millennium Joint Act of Commitment:

- Community, personal integrity,
- A sense of right and wrong,
- Learning, wisdom and love of truth,
- Care and compassion, justice and peace,
- Respect for one another,
- For the earth and its creatures.

We need to find ways of breaking down the barriers which prevent us meeting as human beings. Whatever religion, faith or philosophy we are born into or choose, I believe the experience should make us fully human. It should set us free, and not tie us down. It should be a framework which enables us to become our true selves, open hearted and generous to others.

# Back to the Beginning

At the beginning of this book there is a photograph of the sculpture of the Walking Madonna at Salisbury Cathedral. This is a very powerful symbol, which provokes many questions. Did Mary just visit the cathedral? Will she return? Will she be visiting other places of worship? Does she have an agenda? Is she on a mission? Is she touring the city? Is she meeting important people or will she be open to chance encounters in the streets, the shops and the market places? Wherever she goes, in Salisbury, as in Ipswich, she is likely to encounter people of many faiths and of none.

On the SIFRE board game Diversity, as in this book, we can learn about Bahá'ís, Buddhists, Christians, Hindus, Humanists, Jains, Jews, Muslims, Pagans, Sikhs, Taoists and Zoroastrians, but there are far more people on faith journeys outside those categories than within them. Many people in the UK have dropped out of organised religion while others may be wanting to explore the spiritual dimension of life, perhaps for the first time.

We can read books or google for information, while every day we are presented with opportunities to meet real people from different backgrounds and experiences to our own. Can we greet them with open hearts and minds as fellow travellers on the journey of life? Do we appreciate that we need these encounters for our own growth and maturity?

> "We shall not cease from exploration
> And the end of all our exploring
> Will be to arrive where we started
> And to know the place for the first time!"
>
> *Extract from 'Little Gidding' by T. S. Eliot*

# *Diversity* ©

### *The Game of Inter-Faith and Multi-Cultural Life*

The Game Diversity © has been devised and developed in consultation with members and friends of Suffolk Inter-Faith

Resource. It is a non-competitive board game which enables its players to learn basic information about the faiths now being practised in this country. In addition, it encourages them to look at the appropriateness of statutory systems and processes and to consider the significance of personal encounters within our diverse and fragmented society

The game invites each of its players to assume the identity of someone from a different faith section of society and to experience how that person might feel in daily dealings with fellow members of an ill-informed world. It provides opportunities for discussion of cultural and spiritual issues; and to consider ethical dilemmas.

It is very suitable for the teaching and training of almost all sections of our society; from primary school children to professionals working for the statutory bodies concerned with the welfare and care of our multi-faith and multi-cultural community.

Diversity© comes in a stout A4 sized box with a folding A3 sized playing board. Diversity© costs £30.00 plus £5.00 for postage and packaging.

A 3ft x 3ft playing mat has being developed for use when the game is being used in training sessions. The playing mat (in a cardboard carrying tube) is available at £27.50 plus £5.00 for postage and packaging.

The game Diversity and its component ideas are copyright to Suffolk Inter-Faith Resource. SIFRE ©1999

# *A Handbook of Faiths*

*A Handbook of Faiths* contains sections on the following religious and cultural groups: African Caribbean, Asylum Seekers and Refugees, Baha'is, Buddhists, Chinese, Christians, Hindus, Humanists, Jains, Jews, Muslims, Pagans, Sikhs, South Asians, Spiritualists, Taoists, Traveller Gypsies, Vietnamese and Zoroastrians.

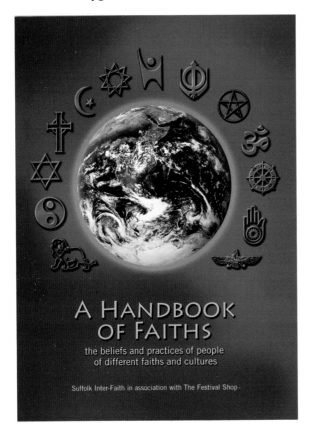

A HANDBOOK OF FAITHS
the beliefs and practices of people
of different faiths and cultures

Suffolk Inter-Faith in association with The Festival Shop

We live in a world of difference - different cultures, different histories, different faiths. Recognising an alternative perspective on the world can open our eyes to fresh ways of seeing things. It can enrich our experience of the world.

I am delighted to welcome the 4th edition of SIFRE's Handbook which provides in a unique and accessible way key information which assists any of us - in communities, in public service, in commercial and social activity - in building and maintaining respectful and good relationships.

Mike More, Chief Executive of Suffolk County Council, November. 2005.

Price: £5.95 (plus 50p p&p)

Both *Diversity* and *A Handbook of Faiths* are available from:

Suffolk Inter-Faith Resource
The Inter-Faith Centre, The West Building,
University Campus Suffolk, Waterfront Building,
Neptune Quay, Ipswich. IP4 1QJ
or Phone 01379 678615 (24 hour answer phone service)
SIFRE is a Limited Company No. 2992865 and a Registered Charity No. 1042612

# Waiting for the last bus home

David and Cynthia came across this picture by Simon Morriss, reproduced on the back cover, when it was on display in the Parish Church in Cirencester and they contacted the artist for his permission to include it. He was delighted to hear how it resonated with SIFRE's work.

**Simon wrote:**

"This painting is a reflection on the discussion between Rowan Williams and Richard Dawkins chaired by Sir Anthony Kenny at the Sheldonian Theatre in Oxford in February 2012.

Fundamentally it is about a conversation. Although anyone who knows something of the views of Richard Dawkins and Rowan Williams will have their own preference, this painting is not about taking sides. Both protagonists are painted in the same way, wearing the same colour and given the same value as an equal part of humanity. The runs of paint in the acrylic indicate the lack of hold we all have on earthly existence and its transitory nature: the last bus a tentative means of reaching an unspecified destination.

However, within the discussion, the meanings ascribed to existence are very different. It is not just the difference between Christianity and atheism, but also perceived incongruities between science and religion and philosophically the difference between materialism and a form of idealism. These underlying assumptions about the world have implications for our lives and the society we create: the conversation is to question them, attempt to make them explicit and understand them as best we can.

I have found the meaning of the painting continues to emerge through interpretation from the process of its creation and beyond, and my hope is that it might act as a primer for dialogue."